Praise for
# A Billion Hours of Good

"This book reached my soul. It's a prescription to leading a life of service that makes all humanity better. Chris reminds us that each of us can make a difference and challenges us to have the discipline to lead a servant-centered life. There is a network effect to helping others that multiplies and creates positive change for the world . . . here is your guide!"

>—**Mark Roenigk,** Head of Hardware Engineering at Facebook,
> Former Technology Advisor to Bill and Melinda Gates Foundation, and
> Director of Taelor's House Foundation

"Chris Field is an astute observer of the human condition. He has used his insights and a lifetime of personal experiences to create a way to leverage the cumulative good in all of us—14 minutes at a time. This book is nothing less than a blueprint for each of us to become a better version of ourselves. He encourages us to embrace our compassion, courage, and creativity. And in this way, he has prepared us to make our individual contributions to *A Billion Hours of Good.*"

>—**Dr. David N. McMurray,** Regents Professor Emeritus,
> Former Peace Corps Volunteer (Kenya), and
> Former Consultant to the World Health Organization

"This book came at just the right time for me. In fact, it is probably just the right time for our world. I found myself smiling and nodding as I quickly turned page after page. Chris Field inspires through excellent story-telling but also provides a practical blueprint for us all to follow. I want to share this book with everyone."

>—**Terri Dorsey,** Director of Executive Development,
> Boys & Girls Clubs of America

"In *A Billion Hours of Good*, Chris pilots a metaphorical lawnmower. He clears a path by anticipating excuses and mowing them over. Chris started with my heart and then nimbly made his way into the part of my brain that too easily generates retorts—and in that very spot he worked his magic. Using pragmatism and relatable stories, Chris showed me I am capable of doing hard things, motivated me to do hard things, and helped me believe in my ability to make a meaningful impact in the world—in just 14 minutes a day."

>—**Corey Oliver,** Former Senior HR leader at Nike and Deloitte

"If you want to make a difference, if you are thinking about the legacy you want to leave, then this book is for you. Chris provides both practical and inspiring tools for making a difference—14 minutes at a time—through his mastery of story. *A Billion Hours of Good* gives us exactly what we need today to generate significant change in the world, wherever we are in our lives and whatever we have to give. The biggest gift and investment we can make is our time. This book teaches us how to spend it wisely. It is incredible how much progress we can make with small increments of time when we commit to being consistent. I'm all in for the Billion Hours of Good movement and for making a difference together. Are you?"

—**Shannon Deer,** PhD, Interim Associate Dean for Undergraduate
Programs, Mays Business School at Texas A&M University

"Have you ever wondered, *What can I do to make a change, and how do I make this change happen to create an impact in the lives of those who need it the most?* Then this book is a must-read for you! Having worked personally with Chris Field in Ghana, I have seen firsthand how his courage, innovation, and compassion are deeply impacting the lives of children and families all over the world. Chris truly believes ordinary people like you and me can change the world—and shows us how to do it. In *A Billion Hours of Good,* not only is Chris inspiring us to become agents of change, but he shares a plan of action that will drive us to make those changes become a reality."

—**Kofi Nyarko,** Program Coordinator at the Harvard Humanitarian
Initiative, Former Country Director at Mercy Project

"With the skills of a true teacher, Chris Field not only inspires readers to live a life of courage, compassion, and creativity, he walks us through specific steps needed to shift our way of seeing the world and then motivates us to put those thoughts into action—driving us to commit just 1 percent of every day to do more good for others. He's delivered a well-structured, practical guide with emotional stories that will shape many a soul, all while fueling a collaborative effort to build *A Billion Hours of Good.* A must-read for anyone wanting to live a meaningful life."

—**Julie Cantrell,** *New York Times* and *USA TODAY* bestselling
author of *Perennials*

# A
# BILLION
# HOURS OF
# GOOD

# A BILLION HOURS OF GOOD

CHANGING
THE WORLD
14 MINUTES
AT A TIME

## CHRIS FIELD

LEAFWOOD
PUBLISHERS
*an imprint of Abilene Christian University Press*

# A BILLION HOURS OF GOOD
*Changing the World 14 Minutes at a Time*

LEAFWOOD
PUBLISHERS
*an imprint of Abilene Christian University Press*

Cataloging-in-Publication Data is on file at the Library of Congress, Washington, DC.

Cover design by ThinkPen Design, LLC
Interior text design by Strong Design, Sandy Armstrong

Leafwood Publishers is an imprint of Abilene Christian University Press
ACU Box 29138
Abilene, Texas 79699

1-877-816-4455
www.leafwoodpublishers.com

21  22  23  24  25  26  27  /  7  6  5  4  3  2  1

*To Dean—the 14 minutes a day you graciously invested in a twentysomething-year-old changed me forever. Your fingerprints are on every good thing I've ever done in ways we'll never understand this side of Heaven. I'm so grateful for you and your life.*

# Contents

# Introduction

This is an invitation. An invitation to reimagine everything you've ever believed to be true about your ability to create authentic and lasting transformation in the world around you.

An invitation to believe you *are* enough and you *have* enough to offer real solutions to the local and global challenges that move you the most.

An invitation to stop waiting weeks, months, and years for all the stars to align (because they never will) and to start living out your biggest hopes and boldest dreams today.

An invitation to stop believing the lie that you need more time and/or money before you can use your passion and talent to make an impact that outlasts your life.

An invitation to start doing the most amount of good possible where you are and with what you have.

This is an invitation. To join a global movement of ordinary people like you and me who want to give back, offer their best gifts, and *do more good* in the world. A collective billion hours of it. Yes, *billion* with a *B*. That's enough good to fill 24 hours a day, 365 days a year, for the next 114,000 years. That's a whole lot of good, and we'll accomplish it together.

You are invited. And it's so good to have you here.

# CHAPTER ONE

# A Case Study
# Named Connor

I first met Connor when the company he worked for hired me to help grow their social media accounts. Connor was their creative guy, and by our second conversation, I realized he was ridiculously talented. Graphic design, video editing, branding, and marketing were his sweet spots, and he oozed brilliance for them all. His was the kind of talent that might feel obnoxious, except Connor also had this infectiously positive and encouraging outlook. Every single email from him started with classic Connor lines like "I hope you're having a killer day" or "Hey, hope your morning is rad so far." He exuded joy and a "sincerely happy to be here" posture that has become all too rare in many companies. Connor is the kind of person I would hire first and then find a job for because he's just that good.

Connor was clearly a happy guy—and for good reason. Mid-twenties, serious girlfriend, a job he loved so much it didn't seem like work, and even time on many weekends to fit in plenty of fly fishing and golfing with his best friend—his dad. It truly felt like Connor had it all.

But one day we were on a call together, and our conversation turned to the subject of human trafficking and the humanitarian work that my wife and I had been doing in Ghana for more than a decade. We'd recently rescued a group of trafficked children and returned them to their families, and I was telling Connor what that meant for those kids and their families, who were now experiencing freedom and new life for the first time. Connor was blown away by the story and made a comment to the effect of "Man, that's gotta be so fulfilling." It was, of course, and still is all these years later, but something about the way Connor said it struck a familiar chord. I'd heard this comment in various forms now for, well, almost a decade. What Connor said was "That must be so fulfilling," but what Connor was thinking was *I would love to make an impact like that.*

> We will do good when we make the conscious decision to do good—and that can happen wherever we are by using whatever resources we have right now.

The good news for Connor, and for you, is that you can. And you will. That's exactly why I wrote this book.

My life's mission is to empower every single person I meet to *do more good* in the world. The greatest lie we tell ourselves is that we will do more good when [fill in the blank with your next big milestone] happens. This is well-intentioned but simply not true. We will do good when we make the conscious decision to do good—and that can happen wherever we are by using whatever resources we have right now.

As we explore this topic, I will uncover three surprising truths for you throughout the following chapters:

1. Most of us believe we have to choose between financial security or making a positive difference in the world. The truth is both are possible, and doing more good will actually make us better at our jobs.
2. Most of us believe we can't accomplish more good because we have limited time and money. The truth is we're hindered not by time or money but by a lack of confidence that fools us into believing we have nothing to offer.
3. Most of us think we are incapable of driving massive impact for good. The truth is we are just one amplification away from improving the lives of thousands of people.

So let's rewind back to my conversation with Connor to see what this looks like in real life. Connor firmly believed all three of the aforementioned falsehoods. He needed to be convinced of the three truths I was suggesting were available to him. I didn't yet have this book to hand him, of course, so instead Connor and I did a miniature version of what I call my "Everyday Activist Makeover." Our conversation looked something like this:

**Me:** Connor, if you were going to do good right now, what do you think that would look like?

**Connor:** I could make a small donation and probably volunteer a couple of times a year somewhere, serving meals, helping at the animal shelter, or something like that.

**Me:** What if I told you that I could teach you how to choose your favorite cause and drive tens of thousands of dollars in donations to them, all while doing what you love most, never asking anyone for money, and in just 14 minutes a day?

**Connor:** I would say, "Yes, please."

So that's exactly what we did. Remember that Connor's very favorite thing, which also happens to be his best gift, is in the realm of graphic design, video editing, branding, and marketing. Connor does this every single day for an incredibly successful company, and he does it at an incredibly high level.

Do you know who needs graphic design, video editing, branding, and marketing work? Pretty much every single charity in the world. The vast majority of nonprofits and charities run on shoestring budgets, which translates to a few passionate and big-hearted people wearing many different hats. Most of these organizations could never afford someone like Connor, but they didn't have to. Connor was willing to work for free if he believed he could make a real difference.

This distinction is critical because Connor, like most successful people, is a high achiever. Redesigning a home page that gets 12 unique visitors a month? *Meh*. Not going to move the needle for him. Creating a full marketing plan with clever messaging, cohesive branding, matching assets for social media, and even a well-polished teaser video to introduce it all to thousands of donors? Now we have Connor's attention, which is good news because the items I just described would be worth tens of thousands of dollars (or more) to a charity with a good reputation, doing good work, and with a need to get an important message out to their donors.

Connor thought the most he could give a charity was a few hundred dollars and maybe a day of his time. Because of that, he was hardly motivated to do anything. But he could not have been more wrong. The opportunity for him to do good and drive massive positive growth and change along the way was right in front of him. He just had to make the choice to start doing good where he was and with what he had—which is exactly what Connor chose to do.

Now the astute reader might be wondering, "Didn't you say 14 minutes a day? How in the world is Connor going to do all that in just 14 minutes a day?"

Well, I'm glad you asked. You see, 14 minutes a day is exactly 1 percent of our day.

Let's do the math: 24 hours × 60 minutes / 100 = 14.4 minutes a day.

If Connor stacked up those 14 minutes a day for one single month, he would have about 7 hours to give to the tasks outlined previously. But since this is a larger project that Connor really believes in, he'll probably be willing to work on it a little longer—say 6 months. If we multiply 7 hours a month times 6 months, this would give Connor 42 hours to help create this marketing plan that will pay back 100 times what he could have donated himself. All while doing what he loves the most—work that doesn't even feel like work.

This is the epitome of starting where you are with what you have. It shows the power of leveraging your very best gifts and talents for the sake of others by donating just 1 percent of your day. And this is precisely how we can collectively join together to give back a billion hours of good.

Connor is a unique guy, but this part of his story is not unique. There are millions more just like him. People like you and people like me. We are young, old, middle-aged, marketers, salespeople, executives, assistants, VPs, artists, teachers, mechanics, stay-at-home moms, computer programmers, managers, retirees, realtors, and a hundred more job titles. Many of us have come to believe that our respective job titles and the roles and responsibilities that come with them restrict us from doing *more good*, but the opposite is actually true. Our unique and varied experiences and job roles do not hold us back but, rather, catapult us forward in using our most exceptional gifts and talents to drive meaningful outcomes.

Can you imagine a world where business consultants help local school districts with teacher turnover issues, where chefs and restaurant owners work together to end food scarcity, where supply chain and logistics personnel create solutions for distribution efficiencies after natural disasters, and where innovators use their creativity to help crack some of the most crushing social challenges facing our communities?

> Our unique and varied experiences and job roles do not hold us back but, rather, catapult us forward in using our most exceptional gifts and talents to drive meaningful outcomes.

I can imagine this world. I want to live in it. I want to help create it. I want to bring it to life in a way that unleashes a global wave of good. And I believe this can be done—but I need your help. And I think you need this as much as the world needs it from you.

Throughout the following chapters. I'm going to show you how to open yourself up to causes you care about (compassion), how to overcome your fears (courage), and how to take those passions and skills that already make you awesome every day and apply them in innovative ways to solve old problems in new ways (creativity). We will then turn your newfound compassion, courage, and creativity into real and meaningful change. All in just 14 minutes a day.

Connor wanted to make an impact. You do too. He has been incredibly successful in his efforts. And so will you. Let's get started.

# A Gift for You

Before we go any further, I want to give you a gift. No, no, I insist. It's the least I can do after you bought this book and made it a priority to sit down and read it. And look! You already made it through Chapter One and started Chapter Two—*woo-hoo*! But there's just one very important rule when it comes to this gift. I don't mean to be difficult, but I'm going to need you to promise me something before I can give it to you: you have to promise that you will not keep this gift. No, *I don't want it back.* That would be rude, and my mother would never let me live that down (and she'll read this book 50 times, so there's no way I could get away with that even if I tried). But you really can't keep this gift—you have to give it away. Deal?

The gift I'm giving you today is the gift of time. It is the most important and priceless gift you could ever receive, because it is one of the very few things money simply cannot buy. But once you receive this gift of time, you have to commit to go out into the

world and give it away—just like we talked about in Chapter One.
Now, remember, we have a deal.

> The gift I'm giving you today is the gift of time. It
> is the most important and priceless gift you
> could ever receive, because it is one of the
> very few things money simply cannot buy.

Today I'm going to give you back 1 percent of your day. But
not just one day—every day. For as long as you live. For most of
us, that means thousands and thousands of total hours. As we discussed in Chapter One, 1 percent of our day breaks down to 14.4
minutes, which we can round down to 14 minutes. I am going to
gift you with an extra 14 minutes each day, with the expectation
that you are going to take that time out into the world and generously give it away to create transformational change both for you
personally and for those with whom you engage along the way.
We are going to use the power of scale to turn your 14 minutes a
day, and that of many others, into a billion hours of good. How
cool is that?

But how exactly am I going to give you the gift of 14 minutes
a day? With a list of 35 of the absolute easiest, simplest, pain-free
(and money-free!) ways for you to start saving that much time
each and every day with absolutely zero negative impact on your
life. Choosing just a few items from this list will save you at least
14 minutes a day. Implementing all these methods would save you
hours each day. Literally. With no change in your quality of life
or work/family productivity. In fact, the opposite case could be
made—almost every bullet point on the list will actually increase
your work productivity and the quality of your family life. Some
of these suggestions are fun, some are more serious, but they're all
legitimate. And they are meant to show you that carving out just 14
minutes from your day is something that we all can easily do with

just the slightest bit of intentionality. So without further ado, start pulling the ribbon on top of that box (I did not wrap this myself, by the way), and let's see what you got . . .

1. Stop hitting the snooze button. Time saved: 5+ minutes
2. Prep your coffeemaker before you go to bed. Time saved: 2 minutes
3. Make coffee at home instead of going to Starbucks. Time saved: 5 minutes
4. Cull your closet to only clothes you like wearing so choosing is easy. Time saved: 5 minutes
5. Leave your keys in a designated place so you're not looking for them every morning. Time saved: 1–5 minutes (Anger saved: Infinite)
6. Buy an automatic water bowl for your dog or cat. Time saved: 1 minute
7. Ask your boss if you can work from home one day a week. Time saved commuting: 5–60 minutes each way
8. Stay in your pajama pants that day, even if you have Zoom meetings. Time saved: 2 minutes
9. Move one meeting each day from in-person to Zoom. Time saved: 10–20 minutes
10. Move one meeting each day from in-person to a phone call. Time saved: 20–30 minutes
11. Move one meeting each day from in-person to email. Time saved: 30–60 minutes
12. Buy a larger coffee cup so you don't have to refill it. Time saved: 2 minutes
13. Bring your lunch to work so you don't have to go out. Time saved: 30–45 minutes
14. Bring your own snacks to work so you don't have to go to the vending machine. Time saved: 5–10 minutes

15. Close your office door and turn your lights off so no one will bother you. Time saved: Hours
16. Stop arguing with coworkers over politics and sports. Time saved: 10–15 minutes (Friendships saved: At least half of them)
17. Check social media only once in the morning and once in the afternoon. Time saved: 20–60 minutes
18. Check email twice a day instead of leaving it open all day. Time saved: 1 to 2 hours
19. Use a calendar availability app to minimize back-and-forth on setting meetings. Time saved: 10–20 minutes
20. Use a web-browser extension to schedule emails so that you can write dozens of emails at one time and schedule them out for the week. Time saved: 30–60 minutes
21. Run an errand on the way home from work. Time saved: 20 minutes
22. Exercise at the same place you drop your kids off for their evening activities. Time saved: 30–60 minutes
23. Limit yourself to one 30-minute TV show every day. Time saved: 30 minutes to 2 hours
24. Pay your bills all at once instead of a couple every few days. Time saved: 10 minutes
25. Set up autopay for bills. Time saved: 10 minutes
26. Cook dinner in a Crock-Pot or Instapot. Time saved: 45–60 minutes
27. Get takeout instead of dining in. Time saved: 30–60 minutes
28. Get dinner delivered. Time saved: 15–20 minutes
29. Make a list and order online only once a week. Time saved: 10 minutes
30. Prep your meals and snacks on Sunday for the following week. Time saved: 60–90 minutes

31. Put your phone in your room when you get home for the day. Time saved: 20–60 minutes
32. No social media at night. Time saved: 30–60 minutes
33. Divide your daily household chores into days of the week so you know exactly what to do each day without thinking about it. Time saved: 10 minutes
34. Teach your kids to manage more chores. Time saved: 10–20 minutes
35. Go to bed just a few minutes earlier. Time saved: 5–30 minutes

I'd like you to go through this list and choose the two or three things you could most easily implement into your daily routine. Underline them, highlight them, or write them down in a place where you'll see them regularly.

Now add up the minutes saved between those two or three (or more) things so you can see exactly how big your gift will be today. (We all know the bigger the box, the better the present. We may grow older, but we never outgrow that belief from Christmases past.)

Anything larger than 14 minutes a day, I want you to keep. Use this time for whatever you want. Learn a new language, read more books, invest more time in your kids, or just take more bubble baths. You deserve it.

But that first 14 minutes, I need you to hold those loosely. The same hands that opened up to receive those 14 minutes need to stay open to now give them away.

Before we go into exactly how you are going to use those 14 minutes a day to create meaningful and transformational change for some of the people who need it most, I first need to convince you of something critically important. That 14 minutes a day is actually enough time to change the world and, by proxy, *your* world.

# Changing the World
# 14 Minutes at a Time

For most of our lives we've been taught, whether explicitly or through implication, that massive, momentous, and headline-worthy events are how the world is changed. This is a lie.

The world is not suddenly changed because a million people gather to protest together. The world is changed because of the work that went into getting those million individuals to believe in something bigger than themselves. The world is changed because organizers now have social proof that lawmakers and elected officials need to listen to them. And the world is changed when those million individuals go home and create micro-changes on a daily basis in their own neighborhoods and communities.

The world is not suddenly changed because an author writes a great book. The world is changed when people choose to read a book and the words take root in someone's heart in a way that changes the way they move through the world.

Changing the world happens one word, one choice, one minute at a time. This is why 14 minutes a day is enough—even more than enough. Because 14 minutes a day becomes nearly 2 hours a week, which becomes more than 7 hours per month, which becomes more than 80 hours per year, which becomes well over 2,000 hours in a 25- to 30-year span. My friend Connor has more than 50 years left, based on the average life expectancy in the United States. His commitment to just 14 minutes a day of good will total more than 4,000 hours during his lifetime—4,000 hours! If Connor took his gifts of marketing and gave them away in 100-hour chunks (a little more than a year at the rate of 14 minutes each day), he would be able to help 40 nonprofits or charities throughout his lifetime. If his work resulted in an average of just ten thousand additional dollars raised for each of those organizations, then he will have been directly responsible for helping create almost half a million dollars of revenue for charitable causes that he cares about. All in just 14 minutes a day.

> Changing the world happens one word,
> one choice, one minute at a time.

So yes. Yes. YES! My answer is a resounding "Yes!!!" when someone asks if the world can really be changed just 14 minutes at a time. It can. It is. And it will continue to be. By Connor, by you, by me, and by many others.

The idea I'm describing here—that a little bit over a long time adds up to a lot—is nothing new. We've all heard of the incredible, almost magical effect of compounding interest when it comes to investing in the stock market, whereby a small bit of money over many years almost always beats much larger amounts over a shorter timeframe. For the most part, this concept has been reserved for financial planning courses or investment advisors. It's almost never applied to how we spend our *time*. We rarely consider the power of compounding anything besides money, which is lunacy because we all wake up with the same 24 hours a day. Thus the playing field is completely leveled each new day.

Leveraging the compounding power of time, when intentionally used, of course, might be the most powerful force of good in the world. Yet we continue to massively underestimate its potential impact while at the same time overestimating the impact of these "once in a decade" type moments that tend to result from a stroke of luck.

Fourteen minutes a day is enough to change our world. That's a fact.

If Connor's 14 minutes a day can help bring $400,000 to charities and another 1,000 people across the world who read this book join him in doing the same thing, then that is $400,000,000. Yes, four hundred million dollars. But it's not just about raising money. It's so much bigger than that. Name any good deed the world needs, and then multiply that hundreds and thousands of times.

Fourteen minutes a day can create thousands of jobs for the most vulnerable.

Fourteen minutes a day can teach millions of children to read.

Fourteen minutes a day can build neighborhoods for low-income families.

Fourteen minutes a day can create, teach, and build any number of real, meaningful, and transformational solutions that absolutely will change the world.

To illustrate the tremendous power of small things adding up over time, consider the story of my friend Lester Banks.

For 29 years now, Lester has worked at Bryan High School in a small town in central Texas. It's the same high school he graduated from many years ago. Now Lester is the head of campus security and also helps the school in many other ways, like selling football tickets and working the concession stand during sporting events—just to name a few. In 1995, Lester created a scholarship to honor his father. He funds the scholarship with proceeds from the snacks he sells in the concession stands and also by putting just a little bit from each paycheck into the scholarship fund. Lester is not a wealthy man. Yet he has now given away more than $50,000 in scholarships to hundreds of deserving students. His scholarship is so popular that 4 out of 5 students in last year's graduating class applied for it. This is the epitome of the 14 minutes a day principle. Many people, myself among them, dream of one day endowing a scholarship. What an incredible way to give back and leave a legacy! But we wait, and wait, and wait, and save, and save, and save, believing it is all or nothing. In doing so, the majority of us will never get around to the things we "wish" but cannot seem to find a way to do. Then there's Lester.

Lester started with a few dollars from each paycheck, aiming to help a few students a year. Now he's given $50,000 in total scholarships. Talk about a legacy. All the more amazing when we consider he is a paraprofessional in an industry notorious for underpaying its employees. Lester Banks believes in the power of hundreds of microdecisions that collectively change the world. So do the hundreds of students he's helped attend college and the thousands more he's inspired.

> My answer is once again a resounding "Yes!" when someone skeptically asks if the world can really be changed just 14 minutes at a time. It can. It is. And it will continue to be.

So yes. My answer is once again a resounding "Yes!" when someone skeptically asks if the world can really be changed just 14 minutes at a time. It can. It is. And it will continue to be. By Connor, by Lester, by you, by me, and by so many others. Millions of others. But it will not happen by accident. It will be a conscious and intentional choice each of us must make. A few minutes at a time. A few dollars at a time. Day by day for the rest of our lives.

The remainder of this book will be divided into two parts. Part I will unpack the topics of compassion and courage—the cornerstones of the inner work that each one of us must do before we go out into the world to share our gifts with others. Because a billion hours of good begins inside of us. If I simply handed you a clever program to follow, it's certainly possible you might carry it out—at least in the short run. But how long can that last before you've moved on to the next big thing, long forgetting the fad you once found yourself so excited by? This is what makes Part I of this book so critical. Part I lays the foundation for the work we want to do every day for the rest of our lives. When we tackle the at-times difficult task of finding compassion within ourselves and then use that compassion to propel us into being more courageous, we are building something that will far outlast any program or plan. This matters because if we just follow someone else's rote directions, we won't take ownership of this crucial life change.

But if the true desire to do good for the world comes from within us and not from someone else, if the good deeds we choose come from our own ideas and not someone else's, if the conviction we have stems from our own hearts and not someone else's, then we'll easily commit to changing the world one good deed at a time. And it all starts in Part I.

Part II is where we'll take the inner work we've done on compassion and courage and learn how to give it away to the world—14 minutes at a time. Each of us gets to choose to use our 14 minutes a day first compassionately, then courageously, and finally creatively to manifest real change. But it all starts with a funny Greek word called *splagchnizomai*.

PART I

# COMPASSION AND COURAGE

# CHAPTER FOUR

# *Splagchnizomai*

A billion hours of good begins with *splagchnizomai*. Now, I've wanted to use this word in a book since the first time I stumbled across it more than a decade ago. Just so you can say it correctly in your head, the phonetic pronunciation would be "splank-kneez-a-my." And this Greek word sounds as awesome as it looks.

There is a famous parable in the Bible about the prodigal son. The story is about a father and his two sons. When the brothers were both young adults still living at home, the younger one went to his father and basically said, "I don't want to wait until you die to get my inheritance. How about you give me my share early, so I can enjoy it now?"

The father, responding with an enormous amount of graciousness, granted his son's request and wished him well.

The young man took the money and ran, moving off for grand adventures. Sadly, he ended up blowing all his inheritance (as most would have expected someone of his age and maturity to do). It wasn't long until the young man had reached a position so desperate and humiliating that he was basically eating the leftover food served to local farm animals. He eventually returned home, where his father greeted him with love and forgiveness (more on this in a minute) and even threw a huge party to celebrate his return.

Seeing what was happening, the older son became furious with the father and refused to come to the party. The father tried to persuade him, but the older brother just could not get over his anger. He could not understand why his selfish, irresponsible, and immature brother was being given such a warm welcome. After all, the older brother had stayed home, cared for his family, shared the workload, and made all the right choices by considering everyone else's needs, while his little brother had thought only of himself.

It's a powerful story—one of my favorites—and is filled with all sorts of beautiful takeaways. So what does it have to do, first, with *splagchnizomai* and, then, with us and our billion hours of good?

*Splagchnizomai* is used in this story to describe what the father felt when he stood on his front porch and "from a long ways off" saw his son returning home. It's translated from Greek into English as the word *compassion*, but it is not the Greek word most commonly used to describe the feeling of compassion. I would go as far as to say that our understanding of the word *compassion* as we use it in the English language does not even come close to describing what the author is trying to convey here in this story.

This funny, long word literally means "to be moved to one's bowels or innards." It is referring to a compassion so fierce and intense that you can literally feel it in your gut. A compassion experienced so acutely that it actually makes your stomach flip-flop, like the moment when the roller coaster tips down after that long, slow clicking uphill. It is the sort of compassion that I believe many of us do everything in our power to avoid because it's very uncomfortable. But this is exactly the kind of compassion that changes the world—because it forces more of a response than "Oh, that's too bad." Compassion that moves us all the way to our core begs us—no, demands us—to respond. Which is exactly why we tend to avoid it. But it is exactly this kind of compassion we must first find and then allow ourselves to fully feel if we're going to live out the good so many of us are hungry to create. Connor will never stick with helping nonprofits with his extraordinary gifts if he does not feel compassion for their mission. Lester would have never faithfully put money aside from each of his modest paychecks if he didn't feel this kind of compassion for students at his school who might need help getting to college.

I was in fourth grade the first time I remember feeling a sense of compassion that went all the way down into my young gut. My paternal grandmother had taken me to El Paso, Texas, to visit my uncle Randy, who worked as a police officer there. For those who may not be familiar, El Paso sits right on the border of Texas and Mexico. At some point during the trip, we went to one particular spot in town where I could actually look across the Rio Grande and see Mexico. I don't know what the view is like now, but my vivid recollection many years later includes a number of small, dilapidated structures with children like me playing together outside of them. We were separated only by the river.

When I asked my grandmother about those structures, I was appalled to learn they were likely the homes of the children playing outside. I immediately felt *splagchnizomai*—compassion that hit me in the gut. My stomach hurt just thinking about the differences between their lives and mine. I was only 10 years old and had no sense of all the social and political reasons a boy like me would have a different life than boys and girls like them, but I remember asking my grandmother a single childlike question: "Can't we just tape money to a rock and throw it to them?" I could not understand why this was not a viable solution. I just knew the feeling in my stomach was very uncomfortable, and the only way I might be able to make it go away was to try and do something, anything to change the disparity I was seeing in front of me.

This would not be the last time I felt this way when seeing a child who lacked some of the basic comforts I took for granted. That little boy visiting El Paso would one day grow up to be a man who would both pick up and throw proverbial rocks at glass houses of injustice. But I did not know that then. I just knew I did not like how my stomach felt that afternoon when we turned and walked away from the Rio Grande.

> I believe we all desire to be filled with a compassion so raw and so real that it makes us feel something—deep down in our guts.

I chose this quirky and hard-to-say Greek word as the title of this chapter because I believe this is the ultimate goal for all of us who desire to engage the world in a way that truly makes it better. I believe we all desire to be filled with a compassion so raw and so real that it makes us feel something—deep down in our guts. But it's just so scary! So unusual, so atypical, so against the norm. This is what makes *splagchnizomai* both so dangerous and so critical. It invites us to run toward the heartache of others instead of away from it. To make ourselves sit in the pain of another person instead of looking away. To feel the hurt and ache of someone else's troubles in such a way that it makes our own stomachs hurt. *Splagchnizomai* is the heart of a billion hours of good because it asks us to care about others as much or even more than we care about ourselves.

This is not simply donating to charity, or flying our flags at half-mast, or putting a bumper sticker on our car, or saying, "Oh, bless them." *Splagchnizomai* reminds us that we might be the "bless" that shows up and sits with "them" in their very worst moment. *Splagchnizomai* is being the kind of friend or even stranger whom others want to call on when they get their worst news. It is a compassion that forces us to crawl into the pit with others because we refuse to walk away. And while the pit is scary and unknown and out of our control, it at least allows us to feel. In a world where we've become experts at numbing our most unpleasant feelings (in a myriad of unhealthy ways), the starting place for a billion hours of good is letting ourselves feel again. It is a quality we seem to have lost in recent years, but one we must commit to finding again if we're going to make the impact we desire.

> *Splagchnizomai* is the heart of a billion hours of good because it asks us to care about others as much or even more than we care about ourselves.

Changing begins with caring.

In a world of headlines, news flashes, text alerts, and unlimited access to instant information, many of us have become desensitized to the pain around us. We have grown so casually accustomed to the suffering of others that our hearts have been anesthetized and our souls sedated. Compassion invites us to do better. To start feeling once again. All the way into our guts.

America changed forever when millions of people watched an 8-minute video of a policeman, whose charge was to serve and protect, instead use his power to kneel on George Floyd's neck while George cried out, "I can't breathe." Making matters worse was that fact that the policeman kneeled there with one hand casually in his pocket while three of his colleagues looked on in silence. A large part of our country lost their collective breath and found themselves gasping for air after watching that video. We felt that collective feeling all the way down in our guts. That sense of compassion burst out of many of us in the form of markers and poster boards and tennis shoes as people gathered across the country (and even around the world) in the largest and most widespread protests and marches since the civil rights movement.

> Compassion invites us to do better. To start feeling once again. All the way into our guts.

When the story broke, we could have closed our eyes, but most refused. Instead, compassion made us ask hard questions about why so many Black Americans feel afraid or why they continue to experience a system that treats them as second-class citizens. For years, Black people have been calling out for change and inviting White people to join in their struggle. But those cries have mostly gone unanswered. It was easier to overlook what was happening, consider it an anomaly, or even worse, suggest that the plight of Black people had no outside or systemic factors. But when these images of George Floyd filled our newsfeeds and airwaves, the truth demanded a compassionate response. We didn't want to watch, but we could no longer simply look away.

Similarly, historians tell us that visibly seeing the pain and suffering of others played a role in one of the most monumental events to take place in America in the last 60 years. In Birmingham, Alabama, in May of 1963, thousands of Black men, women, and children marched for the civil rights that had long been dangled just beyond their grasp. While television cameras rolled, Birmingham police unleashed vicious dogs and high-powered fire hoses on the peaceful protestors. Because of the news cameras, the shocking images of the Black protestors being attacked by dogs and blasted into walls by water hoses made their way into homes across the country. Every evening for nearly a week, news stations across America broadcast the horrific footage as families sat down to watch the evening news together. People across the country were appalled to see for themselves what they had mostly only read in the papers until that point. They demanded a response.

Within days, local business leaders in Birmingham agreed to desegregate lunch counters and dressing rooms, employ more Black Americans, and take down the now-infamous "Whites Only" signs that hung above public bathrooms and water fountains across the city. It was a remarkable turn of events for Birmingham. The civil rights battle was not over and would not be for several more years, but this was a turning point because enough people saw something they would finally admit was wrong and allowed themselves to feel that wrongness all the way down in their guts. They could have turned off their television sets when the footage made them uncomfortable, but the raw footage was not the problem. The problem was a system set up to treat Black Americans as second-class citizens or worse.

Those scenes were shocking to television viewers at home because up until that point, many had never been exposed to such brutally honest coverage. In fact, many people at the time demanded that the television stations stop showing such "horrible scenes." Thankfully, enough stations knew that it was precisely the horrifying nature of the scenes, and the injustice they highlighted, that made them so important to air, so that the bright spotlight of truthfulness could shine completely. By dragging the truth from darkness to light, we allow ourselves to feel true compassion

> By dragging the truth from darkness to light, we allow ourselves to feel true compassion.

It seems nearly every day, we hear news about something awful that has happened in the world—people dying in a tourist bus crash, a mass shooting at a school or church, an overflowing animal shelter, a fire that killed dozens, a flood that caused hundreds of people to lose their homes. Everywhere we turn, there are stories about people suffering. Somewhere along the way, many of us begin to tune these stories out unless they involve us personally. But we do this at our own peril.

Compassion is not a switch we can turn off and on when it is convenient. Feeling something deep in our gut when we encounter hurting people is not as simple as deciding that *this time* we will care. Compassion is a muscle, and this muscle grows by being exercised. We become more compassionate by practicing compassion. We practice compassion by allowing ourselves to see and feel the pain of others. By refusing to choose numbness when we're uncomfortable with hard truths.

Now I am not suggesting that we sit and weep over every single piece of bad news we hear or see or read. That would be both impractical and unhealthy. But if bad news does not even give us pause—if hearing about something awful that has happened does not even muster a pause, a silent prayer, or a hand to our chest in sorrow—then we probably need to ask ourselves why. Why have I stopped allowing myself to feel? When was the last time I allowed compassion to sink all the way into my gut?

If we were watching those scenes from Birmingham today, would we be moved to action by what we saw? What if Birmingham was Minneapolis?

The most important "Birmingham" moment of my life (thus far) took place on a rickety wooden boat in the middle of the world's largest manmade lake, Lake Volta in Ghana, Africa. It was there that I looked into the eyes and held the hand of a young boy named Tomas.

Tomas was about nine years old, dressed in a bright-green shirt as he leaned up and put his arms over the edge of his fishing boat. Tomas was a child slave.

It was my first trip to Ghana, in August of 2009. Just a few months before this trip, I hadn't even known Ghana was a country, and I certainly could not have pointed it out on a map. But then I read a book called *Jantsen's Gift*, in which author Pam Cope details the lives of children from poor families who are trafficked into the Ghanaian fishing industry, where they work long days leading into short nights, only to wake up and do it all over again. Day after day, week after week, month after month, and year after year. Hopeless, dejected, and with no possibility for a future. These children have committed no crime, but they've still been given a life sentence of hardship, with a fishing boat as their holding cell.

Pam's heart-wrenching book caused me to feel something deep in my gut. That's the feeling that first led me to Google her name, contact her, and ask her when I could go to Ghana with her to meet the children myself. That call led me onto a Delta Airlines flight to Ghana, where I stepped onto the tarmac with Pam just a few months later. And that led me onto the rickety wooden boat where I first met Tomas. It was a meeting that would change my life, and eventually the lives of tens of thousands of other people, forever. But I did not know that at the time. Nor did I pick up Pam's book to have my life changed or to change anyone else's life. Regardless, when I allowed myself to feel, all the way into my innards, a deep and pressing compassion, *splagchnizomai* was no longer an idea or theory. It took up residence inside me and made sure I would never be the same again.

A billion hours of good begins with *splagchnizomai*. It starts with rediscovering our compassion so that we will be motivated to action. We will never drive real change if we do not first care. *Splagchnizomai* makes sure we care. All the way into our gut.

# CHAPTER FIVE

# Developing Love
# for Our Neighbors

I returned home from that trip to Ghana with a broken heart. I was no stranger to uncomfortable truths, having spent my college years with the job of directing a summer camp for children from low-income families. But this was a completely different experience. Sitting in a boat and holding the hand of a young child who was owned by another human being and forced to work every day instead of going to school was a fresh sort of pain that forced me to respond.

The day after returning home to Dallas, I can distinctly remember sitting on the couch in our living room crying, weeping even, as I shared with my wife, Stacey, what a beautiful and terrible trip it had been. I had loved almost everything about Ghana—the people, the culture, the songs, the stories, the sights, and the smells. But my time on the lake, with Tomas and other children like him, had been gut-wrenching. I had looked into the eyes of a child in captivity, and I knew I would never be the same again.

It's important to know here that Stacey would have almost certainly been on the trip to Ghana with me, except for the fact that she was six-months pregnant with our first baby. It had taken us almost a year to become pregnant with our first child, and both of us were beyond excited to meet this little one who would be the first to grow our family. One month before I'd boarded the plane to Ghana, we'd found out that we were having a baby girl. (I still feel the butterflies of that moment in my stomach just writing this.) We decided to keep her name a secret from everyone until the day she was born, but we knew we would name her Micah, the prophet in the Bible who penned one of our very favorite verses. It goes something like this: "But what does God really want from people? To act with justice, to love mercy, and to walk humbly with him."

From the time we'd left that doctor's office knowing we were going to have a little girl we would name Micah, we had daily placed our hands on my wife's life-growing belly and yearned that our daughter would grow up to be a woman of justice and mercy. That she would live into and out of her namesake in bold and beautiful ways. Then I found myself home from that trip to Ghana, just a few months before this beloved little girl would be born, weeping on my couch over gross injustices I had now seen and felt personally, deep in my gut. The enduring thought running over and over through my head was this one: "How unfair for me to ask my child to be something I am unwilling to be!"

The months following that first trip to Ghana were some of the most exciting and exhausting of my life. Stacey and I reached out to dozens of our friends and family members, inviting them to join us in helping children like Tomas. The first fundraiser we ever did came together within weeks and consisted of me inviting seven of my friends to join me in taking turns running a team relay from Dallas to Houston (240 total miles). We slept in a borrowed 15-passenger van, didn't shower, ate fast food, borrowed public restrooms, and raised something like $4,000. But it may as well have been $4,000,000 for the way it made us feel. I was hooked.

Six months after the relay, 50 friends gathered with me on a city softball field outside of Dallas, where we broke the Guinness World Record for the longest kickball game in the history of the world. We played kickball nonstop for more than two straight days (50 hours) and, more importantly, raised tens of thousands of dollars to help the children of Ghana.

Just a few months later, I quit my job as a pastor and we started our nonprofit organization dedicated to ending child slavery in Ghana. We named it Mercy Project—a nod to our now infant daughter who had been born the previous December while rare Texas snowflakes floated silently outside the hospital window. The name also put our faith into action, reflecting on our favorite verse in the book of Micah, which we had been reciting throughout Stacey's pregnancy and beyond.

In those first few days after Micah's birth, I'd held her in my arms and all the world seemed to stand still—both from the overwhelming miracle of life that had just burst forth and also from the exhaustion and terror we felt as first-time parents. I looked down at that tiny little baby with a whole lifetime of big dreams and hopes and convictions to come and thought, *Someday you are going to ask me what I did when I learned there were children in the world who were trapped in slavery. I am going to be so proud to tell you I did my very best.*

A billion hours of good starts in our gut—with a feeling we do not allow ourselves to push away. But it must move from there into our hands and feet. A billion hours of good requires us to both feel and then do. Compassion without action is called *empathy*. It is a sincere emotion of sharing the feelings of another person, but empathy alone will never change the world.

Tiny Tomas in that big fishing boat did not merely need someone to share his feelings of desperation and pain. He also needed someone to show up to help him regain his freedom. He needed someone to help him find his way home.

What should we do when we feel deeply, all the way down in our guts, that something in front of us is wrong and needs to made right again? When justice and mercy are missing, how should we respond?

Rather than waiting for someone else to come along and fix the problem, compassion compels us to ask ourselves the question, "Why not me?" Those three words are foundational for a life of a billion hours of good. They compel us forward, believing we both are enough and have enough to make a significant difference in someone's life. That responding with what we have and where we are is a daily decision that requires no special skills or specific resume—only a willingness to constantly respond to the pain around us by asking, "Why not me?"

> Rather than waiting for someone else to come along and fix the problem, compassion compels us to ask ourselves the question, "Why not me?" Those three words are foundational for a life of a billion hours of good.

Children in slavery. Why not me?

Families in my town who are hungry. Why not me?

People without homes. Why not me?

High turnover rates for teachers in low-income schools. Why not me?

Animal shelters filled with pets because of others' irresponsibility. Why not me?

Systemic racism and injustice that affects entire groups for generations. Why not me?

Compassion is love in action. Compassion is as simple as loving our neighbor. And who is our neighbor? Anyone and everyone we will ever meet or encounter.

You mean Mr. Frank who lives next door and has golf-course-worthy grass? Yes.

The crabby woman two streets over whose dog poops on the sidewalk? Yep. Her too.

The teenager who scans my groceries at the supermarket? Indeed.

People all around me and even across the world whose names I'll never know and whose stories I'll never hear? Certainly.

Rich, poor, Black, White, tall, short, big, small, immigrant, politician, and everyone in between? Everyone.

Compassion begins by loving our neighbors, and our neighbors are the people in front of us right now. If you are reading this book in a place where there are other people around you, I want you to look around at their faces. Put the book down and look around at the people you can see from where you sit. These are your neighbors. Whether you know them, do not know them, birthed them, have bled for them, or will never see them again, they are your neighbors.

Loving our neighbor begins with understanding that every single person we will ever meet or encounter or engage with in any way is worthy of receiving love and compassion. Not by someone else who knows them better than we do, but by us. Why? Because they are a human being.

Glennon Doyle says it like this: "I might as well get busy loving the people around me. I'm going to stop trying so hard to decide whether they are the 'right people' for me and just take deep breaths and love my neighbors."

Feeling compassion and then putting that empathy into action is the most straightforward path toward a billion hours of good. To look around and love the people right around us, right now, and then wake up and do the same thing again tomorrow. Choosing to love others well does not happen just all at once—at least not successfully. It's a decision we each have to make with intention, over and over and over again, day in and day out, 14 minutes at a time. It's not always easy, but it's always right. And, in time, it begins to happen much more naturally. Remember, compassion is almost always measured in tablespoons rather than in buckets. That rarely makes the newspapers or goes viral on the internet, but it's true. This is the incredible power of 14 minutes a day. And that truth should give us a sense of freedom because it means we can start where we are, with who we are, and with what we have right now. We all have the choice to love our neighbors with what we have, and that will always be enough.

> Feeling compassion and then putting that empathy into action is the most straightforward path toward a billion hours of good.

People who love their neighbors rarely start that process with some massive act like selling everything they own and giving all their money to the poor. Loving our neighbors can start small, and it can stay small, as long as we run toward people in pain and suffering instead of away from them. When we do this, we begin to view the world around us in a different way. We begin to feel more empowered, more aware, and, often, far kinder.

It's easy to spot someone loving their neighbor. Like the time I was at my favorite coffee shop and a guy dropped the plate of donuts he had just purchased. The manager immediately came rushing all the way across the store. (I don't even know how she heard the glass shatter from that far away.) Instead of showing frustration or even stress, she asked if he was okay, insisted that she'd clean it up, and offered to buy him new donuts to replace the ones he'd dropped on the ground. What a beautiful yet simple act of love. She chose to respond that way. And I highly doubt it was the first time. She had likely been exercising her compassion muscle so regularly that this response probably felt natural and obvious to her. But to the man she served, it was extraordinarily gracious and thoughtful—the sort of moment he will always remember.

> Loving our neighbors can start small, and it can stay small, as long as we run toward people in pain and suffering instead of away from them.

Loving our neighbors does not need to be complicated, but that doesn't necessarily mean it will always be easy either. It will require both intentionality and some degree of selflessness on our part. It will likely cost us at least our time. We'll have to get up from our cozy comfort zones and dare to offer love to others. But that seems a very small price to pay for knowing we are giving the best of the gifts we can offer with no expectation of anything in return.

I can already hear some of you saying, "But we can't just book a flight to Ghana. We can't organize a record-setting kickball game. We can't run a relay across Texas." I understand. Those kinds of actions aren't ideal or reasonable for everyone. But some idea or activity will be. So how can you love your neighbor without having to travel across the world or push your body to extremes? The answer to that question could fill an entire book, but here are just a few ideas to get your brain going (with much, much more of this to come in our later section on creativity):

- We can love our neighbors by dropping cookies off on their porch.
- We can love our neighbors by remembering their big days and calling them.

- We can love our neighbors by sending someone a hand-written note.
- We can love our neighbors by greeting a retail employee by their name.
- We can love our neighbors by asking a stranger how they're really doing and then listening attentively to their answer.
- We can love our neighbors by buying all the flowers from the flower cart and taking them to the residents at a nursing home.
- We can love our neighbors by bringing snacks and drinks to the hospital waiting room and leaving them behind with a note of love.
- We can love our neighbors by pulling in their trash can, taking their runaway dog back home, or mowing their yard when we know they're working overtime.

> The number of ways in which we can love our neighbors is only limited by our creativity and willingness to take the risk of putting ourselves out there.

The number of ways in which we can love our neighbors is only limited by our creativity and willingness to take the risk of putting ourselves out there. People don't always receive our acts of love with gratitude. Usually, this is because we're all so proud that we don't like it when someone gives us something. (Raise your hand if you're guilty.) We can't take it personally when someone feels like that. We certainly want to be sensitive to what others might feel, but we also can't allow that to paralyze us from making neighbor-loving decisions. I wouldn't keep doing the same thing to someone who is clearly annoyed, but I have sought to carry out hundreds of acts like this in my lifetime and can count on one hand the times they've been poorly received.

In the end, we can't control the response of those we choose to show love to. But that shouldn't keep us from loving anyway. And in those moments when it feels like the little bit we're doing just isn't enough, remember these words from my dear friend Becky, who, upon hearing an overwhelmed friend admit her efforts to do good work were "just a tiny drop in an ocean," replied, "Without the drops, there is no ocean."

Tiny drops today, friends. You do yours, I'll do mine, and soon enough we will have an ocean of love. This is the power of a billion hours of good. A collective effort to accomplish far more together than any single one of us could possibly achieve alone. A compelling starting place is remembering that every person we will ever meet is our neighbor, and each one of them is worthy of our kindness and love.

# CHAPTER SIX

# Words
# Create Worlds

One of the most straightforward ways to begin practicing compassion where we are with what we have is through the power of words. Because each and every one of us have the opportunity to share many, many words each day. Potentially powerful and life-changing words.

I was in the barbershop a few years ago when a woman in her sixties came in. "I have cancer," she told the barber closest to the door. "They told me I should cut my hair before I get too far into chemo."

The barber who would be cutting this woman's beautiful, long hair smiled kindly and then pointed at me and said, "Do you want it as short as his?"

Now, you have to understand that I have no hair. None. I saw a picture of myself from behind at age 22 and asked my wife right then and there to shave my head, and I've done the same every week since. As the woman's eyes met mine, I smiled and said, "You have to be pretty good looking to get a haircut like this. But I think you definitely qualify."

Just a few minutes later, all her beautiful hair sat in large clumps on the floor around her chair. I imagine those piles of hair held a lot of sadness for her. As she turned to face the mirror for the first time, I couldn't help but chime in again: "You look absolutely radiant. I'm so impressed you can pull that off so well."

But this time, before she could even respond, I was joined by the two older men both waiting for haircuts of their own. One lowered the newspaper he was reading and said, "Oh, yeah. Looks great, very nice."

The other went even further: "All the girls in Paris are cutting their hair like that," he said in a way that made us all somehow believe he followed Parisian fashion trends. "People will think you're a model from France."

> How much more could each of us take on in the world if we only believed those two things about ourselves— that we are both beautiful and never alone?

The woman smiled and slowly got up to leave. As she walked toward the door, she got a big hug from the barber and a "Good luck," "God bless," and "You can do this" from the few of us lucky enough to bear witness to this divine moment. I know the woman had a long journey ahead of her, and I would imagine she sat in her car that afternoon and had herself a good cry. Much deserved, too, I might add. But I also know her experience in the barbershop that day was different, better, softer, and more tolerable because of the power of words. Words did not take away her cancer or her sadness, but they did remind her that she was beautiful and not alone. And how much more could each of us take on in the world if we only believed those two things about ourselves—that we are both beautiful and never alone?

I wholeheartedly believe that if we each chose to exclusively give our 14 minutes a day to being more thoughtful and intentional with our words, the world would instantly become a remarkably better place for all of us. Yes, action is crucial. But words truly matter too.

The power of words is undeniable, and they are arguably the easiest and most effortless opportunity we have to engage the world for good. Scientists tell us that each one of us speaks between 10,000 and 20,000 words each day.[1] That represents 10,000 to 20,000 chances to speak life, truth, hope, love, light, kindness, goodness, gentleness, joy, and peace into the lives of those we engage each day. We have 10,000 to 20,000 chances to show compassion and build a more beautiful world with the words we speak.

No one seems to know who first coined the poignant phrase "Words create worlds," but I first heard it during college from a professor by the name of Dr. Stephen Johnson. While I really enjoyed his course, those three words are the only part of his class I can specifically remember. But those three words were planted deep in my heart that day and have been nurtured and cultivated in the many years since, in the hope that they will help produce a lifetime of good fruit from my mouth.

> When we speak, our words are not meaningless, futile, or insignificant. Just the opposite. They are full of meaning, potential benefit, and significance,

I believe that words do, in fact, create worlds. When we speak, our words are not meaningless, futile, or insignificant. Just the opposite. They are full of meaning, potential benefit, and significance. Words build up or break apart. Words bless or destroy. But do we truly believe this? Consider the following questions:

- Do we believe the words we speak over our children before school in the morning matter?

- Do we believe the words we speak to the toll collector on the way to work mean something?
- Do we believe the words we speak to the receptionist when we walk into the office have a deep impact?
- Do we really believe the tens of thousands of words we will speak on phone calls and write in emails and send through text messages all day, every day, really have the power to create new worlds?

> In the same way that a brick mason works with stone and mortar and a woodworker uses a lathe, we too are building new worlds every day with the very words we speak.

If we do believe this, and this entire chapter is my impassioned plea that we should, it must change us. It must change the way we speak to one another. It must change the way we write to one another on social media. It must change everything about the ways we communicate with each other. It must change the way we view our potential impact for creating massive good in the world one sentence at a time.

I believe that change will come the day we comprehend that our words are either weapons of mass destruction or instruments of peace. But we have to choose. It will not happen by accident. We must choose words that show we truly care about the people around us more than we do ourselves. Conversation after conversation. Email after email. Text after text. Post or tweet after post or tweet. In the same way that a brick mason works with stone and mortar and a woodworker uses a lathe, we too are building new worlds every day with the very words we speak. What a sacred commission.

Let's imagine that each day when we wake, we have a never-ending stack of one-hundred-dollar bills. Our job is to go into the world and give away that money. We'll never run out of cash, and there's no limit to the amount we can give away. Everyone can receive as much as they need, and there will always be plenty for the next person we meet.

That's how it is with our words. There is no finite amount of the gentle and kind words we're allowed to give away. We can embrace the vibe of Oprah Winfrey and scream at the top of our lungs, "You get a kind word, and you get a kind word, and you get a kind word!" We can offer the people in our lives a buffet of kind and truthful words, much like the food available on cruise ships. The supply will never end.

We can start with an appetizer of affection, follow it up an entrée of encouragement, top it off with some generosity of spirit, and finish with a nightcap of delight. Still not satisfied? Not to worry, we always have affirmation, gentleness, and inspiration available for those who need a little extra. There is truly no limit to the amount of good our words can do, so why do we not use them to create great, big, giant worlds of goodness every single day?

I believe it's because we do not really believe that our words create worlds.

> We underestimate the power of a kind word, and we underestimate the power of an unkind word—both at our own peril and the peril of those around us.

We underestimate the power of a kind word, and we underestimate the power of an unkind word—both at our own peril and the peril of those around us.

"Sticks and stones may break my bones, but words will never hurt me." We've all heard that common childhood jingle, but it might be the most untrue of them all. I have a feeling that you, like me, have long forgotten the throb from a punch or push you once received, but I bet you can still recall the sting of an unkind word spoken to or about you. I certainly can. Because words really do matter.

Hurtful words break something inside of us that might take years to repair and likely will never be forgotten. Kind and gentle words do the opposite. Kind and gentle words are a healing balm in a world of tearing down, breaking, and destroying, which is why they feel so refreshing when do they come.

My wife and I have four young kids. They are currently between the ages of three and ten years old. If you do not have children, or you do not have as many children as we have, I want to explain to you what going to a restaurant with four young children is like. Going to a sit-down restaurant with four young children feels a bit like being placed in the ring of a circus, on stage at a comedy show, or on the seat of a dunking booth, where at any moment someone could hit the target and cause you to crash into the water. The way you sit on the edge of your seat in a dunking booth, just waiting for the inevitable to happen, is the same way you sit on the edge of your seat at the table when you are a parent with four young children at a restaurant. It is not a matter of if the fall will come, but how often and how quickly you'll take that plunge. My strategy is to always expect the fall so that I'm not disappointed or surprised when it does inevitably happen.

One night, we were out at a restaurant, juggling food prep and spilled drinks and crying babies and silverware falling on the ground and the whole shebang, when a woman walked up to our table. She seemed close in age to our parents, and she wore a knowing smile on her face. It seemed clear this woman was a mom, and I was betting she knew the edge-of-the-dunking-booth-seat feeling herself. That made it all the more meaningful when she leaned down between two frazzled parents and said five words I can still remember all these years later: "You have a beautiful family."

She did not have to say that. I'm sure we had interrupted her peaceful night out with her spouse. But she went out of her way to show us compassion by speaking those words. She did not just think them; she gave voice to them. She didn't say them quietly to her husband; she said them aloud to us. It made our night, and we have never forgotten that gentle kindness from a stranger. Words create worlds.

Words are an obvious and powerful tool in our journey to bring a billion hours of good to the world because words convey much more than what is actually being said. For example, when we leave a surprise sticky note on our partner's mirror that says "I love you," or when we drop a random text to a friend that says "I'm thinking of you," or when we email a colleague out of the blue to say, "You've been working so hard on this project and I see you," the world these words create goes far beyond the actual letters we write. What the other person reads, what they hear, and what they feel are all completely different things and all much more significant than the words themselves.

> A single sentence delivered in the right way at the right time has the chance to completely change someone's day for the better—perhaps even their entire outlook!

They may read the simple words we wrote, but what they will hear is our care and concern for them. They'll feel like we saw them where they are, which reminds them they are not alone in the world. This is the power of words. A single sentence delivered in the right way at the right time has the chance to completely change someone's day for the better—perhaps even their entire outlook! All around us are people barely hanging on for dear life, and our words have the power to either pull them away from the ledge or push them over. Let us commit to being people who will use our words to draw people away from the ledge instead of shoving them over.

In this age of technology and convenience, we are able to connect with each other more quickly and easily than ever before. But we are often so busy that we fail to do so. It stays on our mental to-do list for days until it eventually gets pushed off by a new task. My best counsel is to send that text or email or write that note right when you think about it. Get in the habit of immediately responding to that nudge from within you that says, "I bet this person is feeling down or alone today. I should say something to them." Yes, we should! Right now.

Every single day, I try to text or call someone I love and care about just to say, "Hey, you're important to me." I don't need to have a specific reason to say that—in fact, it's almost more powerful if I do not have a specific reason. Just randomly showing up and offering them the gift of kind words is enough. I do this because I know how it feels when someone does it for me. I do this because I believe in the world-creating power of words. I do this because I believe words are the easiest and most painless opportunity we have to show compassion to those around us. They also give us a simple way to work together and bring a billion hours of good to the world. If we choose to use our extra 14 minutes a day to make others feel more seen, heard, and valued by way of our words, then that alone will be enough to create real and lasting change.

## NOTE

[1]Richard Knox, "Study: Men Talk Just as Much as Women," NPR, July 5, 2007, www.npr.org/templates/story/story.php?storyId=11762186.

CHAPTER
SEVEN

# The
# "Other"

One of the most important parts of making the intentional decision to join the billion hours of good movement is to realize that we don't know what we don't know, and we can't see who we can't see. Let me explain with a story.

"Do you know the names of the janitors who work at your school?" This was the question I posed one day to the teenagers at church. I'd been working with them every week during the very beginning of my early adult life. As a mostly White, mostly middle-class youth group, we would often discuss how our social blindness kept us from seeing those people around us who were often hidden in plain sight. Janitors are not really hidden, of course, but they have the sort of job that is far too often ignored, unappreciated, and sometimes even dishonored—especially during those angst-filled teenage years, when much of the focus seems to be on merely surviving the cruel hallways of junior high and high school. I hoped that if these young people walked into their respective schools and began actively looking for their janitors, they would begin to see other hidden people too. Cafeteria workers, aides, bus drivers, even some of their peers who existed in plain sight but would occasionally go through an entire school day without anyone speaking to them.

> It seems those who are most often unseen make for some of the most loyal and gracious friends.

The first time I asked this question of my teenagers was fairly uncomfortable. Very few of them could say "Yes." I lightened the mood by assuring them that I absolutely, positively could have never named the janitors during my junior high and high school years—mostly because I was kind of a selfish jerk back then. My young friends heard me and took heart. Within just a few weeks, they began coming back to the group not only with stories of their janitors' names but also with stories of budding new friendships. It seems those who are most often unseen make for some of the most loyal and gracious friends.

"Do you know your janitor's name?" is not really a question about janitors at all. It is a question about how we look at the world. For better or worse, most of us see what we want to see. So being people who know our janitors' names means we are much more likely to see and engage other people we might have ignored before as well. In a society that tends to target people whose lives exist outside the culture's false view of what's "ideal," we're all surrounded by people whose job titles, socioeconomic status, education level, sexual orientation, or ethnicity make them seem "other" from us. And we've been conditioned to fear anything "other" than us. I do not believe we do this on purpose, but we often live in an echo chamber, validating our distorted belief that the way we experience the world is the way everyone experiences the world. This is not only untrue but dangerous.

Joining forces to do a billion hours of good compels us to actively seek out the "others" in our lives and not just learn their names but begin real relationships with them—even if those relationships start just 14 minutes at a time. Compassion compels us to care about the "other" because we understand that our own worldview and perspective is limited.

Engaging the "other" is an act of compassion, but not in the way many of us might first think. Our tendency (myself included) is to believe that the "other" might need or want our help. Maybe we can meet this person so unlike us and share our food, or clothes, or money with them. Maybe they need a sleeping bag or even a camping oven. Whatever they need, we can provide it. That's what many of us do best—find a project, solve the problem, and move on to the next person. But we cannot make the mistake of confusing problem solving for compassion. That kind of belief often comes from a place of pity and or even personal piety or superiority. That's not our goal. Engaging the "other" is not a gift because of what it gives to them but because of what it does to us—inside of us, to be more precise. When we engage the "other" by forming real relationships, we begin to realize how narrow and restrictive our view of the world truly can be.

> When we engage the "other" by forming real relationships, we begin to realize how narrow and restrictive our view of the world truly can be.

To use an example that will thrill my piano teacher (more on this soon), it's as if we've been playing single notes on the piano and feeling like that sounds pretty darn good, and then we engage the "other," which allows us to discover chords. And wow—these "other" sounds are game changers! We cannot appreciate that lovely music until we hear it, and we cannot appreciate all the beauty and diversity the world has to offer until we sincerely engage with those we once saw as being different than us—the "other."

Ultimately, this becomes a way of showing compassion to ourselves because it ushers in a level of freedom and expression we might have otherwise never known. Let me say it another way: Engaging the "other" and believing we're doing them the true favor is like us believing we're doing an author of a great poem a favor by reading it. If the poem is truly great, we're the benefactors more than the author! But not if the whole time we're reading it we feel as though we're doing them generous service.

My three oldest kids have all traveled to Ghana with us now. They were four, five, and seven years old at the time of their travels. You might imagine that more than 24 hours of travel by car, plane, taxi, and then boat would not be the most enjoyable prospect for parents of such young children. We thought we might hack the long travel by giving our kids new apps and extended time on an iPad (which we typically restrict considerably), but that plan failed when one of our kids became so engrossed with the new app that he peed in his pants before we'd even finished our first three-hour flight! The reason we wanted to take our kids all the way to Ghana, brutal travel and all, was to introduce them to a new place filled with people they probably believed were quite different from them. We wanted our kids to see and feel from a young age that the world was both enormous and not actually that big at all.

Yes, it took us a long time to get there, but we could buy a plane ticket and be on a far-away continent when we woke up the next day. How amazing is that? Yes, their skin tones and words and foods and houses might have appeared different from ours, but their games and laughter and smiles and humanity were exactly the same. Our lives may have looked different on the surface, but we were similar in all the ways that mattered most. These are the sorts of things you can only learn by engaging the "other," and it's important to do so on their terms, not ours.

I remember one afternoon in Ghana when it began to rain. We all took cover underneath the one solid, aluminum roof in the entire village—the church. This was a small fishing community with only a few hundred people, and most of the children did not attend school, so they followed us to safety from the storm. My son was five years old at the time and didn't know a single word of their native language (I only knew a few), but he joined the other children to play while the rain pitter-pattered on that metal roof for what felt like hours.

In the ways that matter the most to kids, they had everything in common. This is what being with the "other" will help us do. It will help us gain perspectives that we could not have developed otherwise. After all, it's one thing to learn about children in another country by reading about them in a book. It's something altogether different to dance with them on the dirt floor of their church while your laughter fills the room and overflows through the open windows.

> Engaging with the "other" teaches us,
> guides us, humbles us, focuses us, and
> makes us both more grateful and kind.

Engaging with the "other" teaches us, guides us, humbles us, focuses us, and makes us both more grateful and kind. Sincere empathy is often born out of those relationships that change our worldview. I find that conversations about difficult and sometimes controversial subjects are profoundly different when we're talking about real experiences and not something we read in the newspaper or saw on the internet. "I know a guy who said" does not carry with it the same weight, wisdom, or sensitivity as "my friend Susan said." But we will never know Susan's important story if we do not first have a relationship with Susan. And if all the "Susans" in our life think and look and act just like us, then we'll quickly run out of new things to learn. In turn, we'll remain fairly shallow and one-dimensional. This is why it is so wrong to view the "other" as someone we can rescue, because the truth is, in most cases, we're the ones being rescued from the cage of our own small-mindedness.

As a brief aside, there may be no place where this kind of thinking happens more often than the echo chambers we call social media. A number of recent articles and documentaries seem to point to an intentional algorithm-driven polarization of Americans, especially when it comes to hot-button issues such as political elections.

It is not difficult to understand how dangerous this can be when we primarily listen to those who think and act and look like us. The implications of that, at the very minimum, lead to our false beliefs that our opinions are the only reasonable way of viewing the world.

This, of course, means that those who do not agree with us are ignorant fools—a view that is dangerous, crippling, arrogant, and sadly all too common. We must fight against this proactively, and I can think of no better way to do that than using our 14 minutes a day to engage people who are different from us, reminding ourselves of our shared humanity.

In the end, we are all so much more alike than we are different. But engaging the "other" is the only way to learn this.

Our lives are filled with "others." But do we see them? I want to circle back to the question I asked that group of teenagers at the beginning of this chapter: "Do you know the name of your janitors?" If so, great. But how do we now go beyond that? Do we know anything about their families, their stories, their hopes and dreams and fears? There is a distinction here that I believe is important for us to make: Having a friend is not the same as being a friend. I have recently been convicted of this truth in my own life.

I'd been doing some serious soul searching during a morning run (which is when I do my best thinking and reflection). That morning, I had an epiphany: I am friends *to* many people different than me but not friends *with* them. Let me explain.

Being a friend *to* the "other" puts us in full control of the relationship. Typically, it looks like us filling a need for them on our timing and according to our schedule. The power in the relationship is very much on our side because we have all the control. Both parties feel this one-sided power, by the way, and it completely changes the dynamics of the relationship. But being friends *with* the other is actually a legitimate and mutually beneficial friendship. It is not predicated on one person needing something from the other person, and there is no imbalance of power. Instead, the friendship is based on a true partnership in which both parties benefit from sharing their skills, talents, love, and care for one another. This is a true friendship with the "other," and it is by far the most compassionate way we could seek to be in a relationship.

Brené Brown says: "Compassion is not a relationship between the healer and the wounded. It's a relationship between equals. Only when we know our own darkness well can we be present with the darkness of others. Compassion becomes real when we recognize our shared humanity."

> Being a friend *with* the other is the noble calling we should be seeking to live into.

Being a friend *to* the "other" is a very low bar and often (even if unintentionally) does more harm than good because of the imbalance of power. I can assure you I have felt the sting of this sort of relationship firsthand, most often as the one with the power. Being a friend *with* the other is the noble calling we should be seeking to live into. That is where true compassion lives, both to one another in the real relationship and also to ourselves, because these are the kinds of relationships that cause us to grow and improve.

When you think about your own relationships with the "others" in your life, what do they look like? Are you frequently engaged with people who look, think, work, vote, pray, and spend differently than you do? If not, why not? If so, are you friends *to* them or *with* them? Is your relationship based on charity or cherished togetherness?

Such questions and relationships can certainly produce both hard and uncomfortable conversations. I have felt the weight of the lack of these kinds of relationships even while writing this chapter. The truth is that in my own life, I have become better than average at being friends "to" the other, but I have an extraordinarily long way to go when it comes to being friends "with" the others in my life. Maybe you do too. A billion hours of good means making the conscious decision, to ourselves, that we want to do better. That we will start with seeing the "others" in our life, but we will not stop there. We will aim to build true and lasting relationships *with* them as well—experiencing the unique gifts of their lives and celebrating our shared commonalities until we no longer see anyone as "other" at all.

# CHAPTER EIGHT

# Turning Walls into Tables

America learned the name Ahmaud Arbery in May 2020. Unfortunately, we will never get to know him beyond his name because he was murdered by two vigilantes. As our country has grieved the senseless death of another young person of color, we have, again, raised a number of uncomfortable and difficult questions on the topics of systemic racism and injustice in America. As has become the norm, these conversations have primarily played out on social media, where people who have never even met in real life, much less shared a meal together, are making judgments about each other's values from 280-character posts on small screens they hold in their hands. I am guilty of this, and you probably are too. While social media can certainly be used for good, I worry that it is building walls between us rather than uniting us.

What if we used our 14 minutes of good a day to turn those walls into tables?

You may have heard this familiar saying, especially in our recent political climate, with people calling for us to build tables, not walls. I want to extend this concept even further. At a time when we will throw everything we've ever known to be true about another person out the window based on one sentence or a single differing view, it is more critical than ever that we consciously make the compassion-led decision to build bigger tables, where all are welcome, instead of taller walls, where few can pass.

> The words we say to one another, and more importantly the manner and fashion in which we say them, are the factors that make or break any experience.

The irony is that many of the materials required to build a table and a wall are the same. A table is really just a wall that has been turned on its side and surrounded by chairs. And that is exactly what must happen for us to begin moving forward together in hard conversations, in relationships, and when learning how to agree to disagree without being spiteful. We must figuratively turn the walls we've built to keep others out into tables we've set to bring us together.

Something special happens when we sit around a table and share a meal together. There is a togetherness and a mutual experience that goes far beyond the actual place settings and foods. It's not about the silverware or centerpieces or perfectly cooked casseroles. It's about what we learn and how we're changed by gathering with each other. It's about the company and the conversations.

You may immediately associate the idea of a Thanksgiving meal with your family with feelings that are good, bad, or somewhere in the middle. These feelings have almost nothing to do with the quality of the food you ate and everything to do with the way the people sitting around that table made you feel. We may joke about how Dad always overcooks the turkey or how our sister-in-law made the sweet potatoes with the consistency of a smoothie, but what we really remember is how safe, loved, and welcome we felt when we pulled up our chair and set our napkin into our laps. The words we say to one another, and more importantly the manner and fashion in which we say them, are the factors that make or break any experience.

If your family is anything like mine, you know there is almost no chance that everyone sitting at the table together will agree on every topic. My family's Thanksgiving table includes people of different ethnic backgrounds, political parties, and far different income categories. We've got hunters sitting by vegetarians, Trump voters next to "anybody but Trump" voters, electric car drivers next to oil and gas executives, and Black Lives Matter supporters next to policemen. Yes, I'm serious. But never once has our family Thanksgiving ended with people storming off angrily or throwing my mom's famous dinner rolls at one another. There have certainly been some passionate conversations, and sometimes "Let's agree to disagree" is the best way to move forward, but something magical happens when we sit around the table and look one another in the eye, rather than yelling at each other across the internet or typing in ALL CAPS WITH EXTRA EXCLAMATION MARKS ON FACEBOOK!!!

> Sitting around a table together changes the way we look at one another because we're actually forced to sit there and look at one another.

Sitting around a table together changes the way we look at one another because we're actually forced to sit there and look at one another. When we "break bread" together, a practice that dates back to the beginning of time, we share far more than food. We share our lives and conversations and, yes, even that bowl of green beans. And by opening ourselves up to that level of intimate togetherness and connectedness, we remember our shared humanity.

In June 2015, a young White man entered a historically Black church in Charleston, South Carolina, and killed nine people. In subsequent confessions, he told police that his attacks were racially motivated.[1] As newsfeeds and blogs filled with conversations about racism and injustice, there was an all-too-common tendency to dismiss people with opposing views as stupid, unreasonable, or worse. Everyone was talking, but it seemed no one was listening to all the words being said.

I was on a run one morning, right in the middle of all this conflict, and I found myself deeply troubled by the hard, messy, and difficult conversations that had taken place in our country over the past weeks. I was saddened by the pain that words can bring, and I was saddened by my role in speaking some of those hurtful words. As I ran, and lamented, and thought about a better way forward, a vibrant vision came into my head—one that has everything to do with turning walls into tables.

In that vision, I saw two people in disagreement. Whatever it was they were disagreeing about, it seemed important to both of them. They were each sure they were right. Neither was happy with the other, and it was hard for them to imagine what might happen next. But then a table appeared. A simple wooden table with a simple wooden chair on each side.

The two sat. They did not speak, but they simultaneously reached across the table and took the other person's hands into their own. Still not speaking, they began to look deep into one another's eyes. When they did this, they began to imagine all the different things those eyes had seen and read. A lifetime of sights and words were living behind those eyes. Then they moved onto the ears and began to consider all the things those ears had heard.

Good, bad, hard, and sweet words. A lifetime of words. Some building the person up but many tearing them down.

Their attention then shifted to the chest. The centerpiece of the entire human body. If they focused, they could barely perceive the gentle breathing, in and out, in and out, of their lungs. They realized that in that moment, they were sharing the same air, and that the shared air was keeping them both alive.

Finally, they considered the hands they were holding. The callouses, the wrinkles, the softness, and the rough parts. They considered the babies these hands had cradled. The times these hands had come together in prayer. The lovers these hands had gripped. The dying mothers these hands had held. There were entire lifetimes in those hands. Hands that had created something out of nothing. That had held the deepest pains and the greatest joys.

Slowly, or maybe quickly, the issue between them no longer seemed like such a big deal. They hadn't changed their opinions, but their stance suddenly paled in comparison to their shared humanity. It disappeared into the truth of who they were in that very moment, who they'd been, and who they wanted to be. And so they let go. They never spoke a word. But they said everything. And they no longer felt the need to be right. Because their shared humanity was enough. And from that moment on, it always would be.

> When we stop long enough to look into the eyes of another human being, we are reminded that we are so much more alike than we are different.

This is the potential power that the table holds to serve as a place of connection, reconciliation, and abundance. When we come out from behind our screens, when we unlock our front doors and walk out into the yard, when we gather together in the coffee shop or for brunch, we make ourselves available for transformation that is unlikely to happen otherwise. When we stop long enough to look into the eyes of another human being, we are reminded that we are so much more alike than we are different.

When we sit together and share our hearts and dreams and hopes and fears, something softens inside of us. In rural Ghana, where Mercy Project does our work, there is a beautiful tradition that takes place every time visitors come into a village for the first time. Everyone, both locals and the new visitors, gathers under a large mango tree for the meeting. The purpose of the meeting is simple: The villagers want to hear (1) where the visitors have been, and (2) where the visitors are going. This is their polite way of saying, "We can better understand why you're here if you tell us where you've been and where you plan to go next."

> This is an invitation for us to start naming our shared longing to belong and then adding seats at our tables to bring that longing to life.

This kind of story sharing is what drives deep connection between us. Our capacity for empathy explodes when we see beyond the person in front of us and remember they are as fragile, broken, and hopeful as we are. I can't help but wonder what our world would look like if we all began using this simple question in our own lives. To hear one another's stories. Where we've been, and where we're going. To listen. To learn. To share our most important calling: being human together.

Somewhere deep within each of us is a longing to belong, to be known, and to be loved. I've never forgotten a line I read one day on a "Humans of New York" story on Facebook: "At every moment we are either showing love or crying out for it." Sadly, our fears and insecurities often keep us from acknowledging this desire, much less actually pursuing it. So we fill that void with all sorts of alternatives—usually unhealthy things.

We overfill our plates, brains, calendars, and bank accounts in an attempt to ignore this deep truth that we're too scared to name. But it's there, in the dark of the night. It's lurking when we don't get that email back. It's right around the corner when our spouse doesn't seem to hear us. It's hiding nearby when our friends forget our important day.

It's okay for us to want to be known. To want to belong. But the only way for that to happen is for us to start sitting around tables together with open hearts and open minds. To be with one another through the good stuff and the bad. To move through life with one another deeply and beautifully and messily and fully. This is an invitation for us to start naming our shared longing to belong and then adding seats at our tables to bring that longing to life.

Tables come in all different sizes. Our goal should be to build the biggest tables we can possibly squeeze into our lives. We should seek to be people who live by these words: There is always room at our table for one more chair. Because the table won't be the same without that extra voice, viewpoint, and lived experience. We need to hear everyone's stories, jokes, and tears to better understand our own.

> There is always room at our table for one more chair.

There is always room at our table for one more chair because we don't know what we don't know, and we never will unless our tables get bigger. So grab whatever chair you can find, from whatever room you can find it in—even go out to the garage if you have to grab a camping chair. Just make sure there's always room at the table for one more person. Always.

One day, my wife came home from shopping at Target and told me I just had to see something she'd found. Let me confess that I generally feel less enthused about whatever her new find might be than she is, but in this particular case, I shared her joy. It was a new doormat for our front porch that read: "All Are Welcome Here." Wherever you've been, whatever you've done, whatever we agree or disagree on, all are welcome here. This is the message we want our lives to announce.

I remember when my wife and I lived just outside Dallas in our early twenties, and Chili's was one of our favorite date-night spots. (Don't judge us—Chili's was *the* spot to be back in the early 2000s.) We went there a few times a month, and during our visits, we got to know some of the regular waitstaff. I had a practice at the time of leaving a business card with our tip and writing a quick note on the back to the effect of: "Save this and call me if you ever need anything."

One day I was at work when I saw a number I didn't recognize on my cellphone. I answered and heard a man's voice on the other end who identified himself as Ivan. To be honest, I didn't think I knew anyone named Ivan, so I was ready to politely move on, but then he mentioned saving my business card from when he was our waiter at Chili's. It turns out Ivan and his fiancée were getting married soon. Like, 10 days away soon, and they didn't have anyone to officiate the wedding. Ivan sheepishly admitted he'd been given the job of finding an officiant months ago but had totally dropped the ball. They were desperate, and he wanted to know if I could help.

I was happy to help, and meeting their families and officiating their wedding just 10 days later turned out to be an absolute joy—a joy I would have never been able to experience if I had not chosen to see Ivan and make myself seen to him. I would have missed this relationship if I had not intentionally been looking for people who might want to pull a chair up and join us at our table.

When we open our arms and homes and tables to people we don't know, or don't like, or don't look like, it's not simply a kind gesture. It changes something in us. When we announce to the world that we always have room for one more chair, a funny thing begins to happen—people actually start showing up. The world is so hungry and desperate for this authentic connection that when we make ourselves available, it is almost a certainty that someone is going to take us up on that offer. What a gift that is for all involved.

> When we announce to the world that we always have room for one more chair, a funny thing begins to happen—people actually start showing up.

Can we actually turn walls into tables in just 14 minutes a day? Absolutely. Should we? I think we must. Sometimes a billion hours of good starts with pulling just one more chair up to the table.

If we were only known for one single part of our lives, may it be this: I don't have to agree with you politically, religiously, or in any other way to make myself available if you ever need me. Call on me, and I'll be there. Whether broken, excited, hopeful, or hurt—doesn't matter to me. I'll come to a bar, a hospital room, or your house. And you will always have a seat at my table.

### NOTE

[1] Matt Zapotosky, "Charleston Church Shooter: 'I would like to make it crystal clear, I do not regret what I did,'" *Washington Post*, January 4, 2017, www.washingtonpost.com/world/national-security/charleston-church-shooter-i-would-like-to-make-it-crystal-clear-i-do-not-regret-what-i-did/2017/01/04/05b0061e-d1da-11e6-a783-cd3fa950f2fd_story.html.

# Gabe and the Domino Effect of Good

I walked into the post office one day and found myself in a line that stretched nearly to the door. I don't know when you last visited your local post office, but I generally do not find it to be a place where people show up excited and happy about life—even more so when standing in a line 15 people deep. In some post offices, a line that long could easily turn into a half-day affair!

I immediately spotted a mom with her young son, and it was clear from the various boxes and papers in her hands (not to mention the look on her face) that they'd already been there for a while, preparing her packages. Now she was going to have to wait in the long line, with an already bored kid, surrounded by impatient people. What could go wrong?

But this is when the magic happened.

As the mom got into line, and her son (we quickly learned his name was Gabe) made it clear he was not happy about standing in line, an older gentleman pointed to an old penny on the ground.

With Mom's permission, Gabe picked it up. The man explained that it was a lucky penny and that Gabe should take it home. The boy grinned and stuffed it proudly into his pocket.

An older woman took the next turn and started talking to Gabe about how old he was. He proudly held up an entire hand full of fingers, and the woman could have won an Oscar for her performance in acting surprised that such a big and handsome boy was only five years old. Gabe smiled even bigger than when he'd found the lucky penny.

As that conversation ended, it was my turn. I spotted a couple of abandoned boxes someone had left behind and brought them over near Gabe and his mom. After a smile and subtle nod from his mother, I said, "Gabe, do you know what these are?"

He shook his head shyly.

"These are boats. And you can pretend this whole floor is a huge ocean. And you can ride in your boat all the way to the end of the ocean where your mom will talk to the workers. How does that sound, Captain?"

Gabe crawled in quickly and began his adventure without even answering. The whole line was now watching and smiling and remembering how meaningful it feels to be seen and to see others.

The mother looked like she was about to cry out of gratitude. And Gabe? Well, he was busy fighting off pirates.

> When we see others act generously, love lavishly, and choose compassion, it compels us to do the same.

This is the power of a billion hours of good to create a domino effect. One man in a busy post office takes just a single moment and a little social risk and points out a lucky penny. The rest is pirate ship history. When we see others act generously, love lavishly, and choose compassion, it compels us to do the same.

Each one of us can choose to start a domino effect of good. Moment by moment, day by day. And when we do make that choice, we can trust that others are watching and taking our cue. This is the domino effect of a billion hours of good.

When someone speaks a kind word to us, we are more likely to speak a kind word to the next person we encounter.

When someone gives us the benefit of the doubt, we are more likely to extend that same grace to the next person we engage.

When someone moves over to make space for us at their table, we are more likely to watch over our shoulders for the next person who might need a seat.

Because compassion begets compassion.

The most beautiful and hard-to-believe part about all this is that we have no idea where this domino effect will go next because we don't get to see that part of the story. I have thought about the story of Gabe and his mom every single time I've been in the post office since then. Don't you think at least a few of the other people in line that day have done the same? The first domino that day was a frazzled mom, a little boy, and a shiny penny on the ground. The last domino from that simple act might stretch out for hundreds of years. We simply cannot know. But we do know this: no subsequent domino will ever fall without the first domino falling. That is a fact.

Several years ago, I was invited to speak to a group of high school seniors who would all be entering Texas A&M University (where I am a lecturer) the following fall. This group was unique in that it was made up entirely of first-generation college students. My charge to them that morning was to offer a mix of cheerleading and challenges. Some "I'm proud of you" with a healthy dose of "It's time to start believing you have the gifts to change the world." In that speech, I spoke briefly about our work with Mercy Project in Ghana and how challenging and fulfilling it was to pursue such a meaningful task. This was in our first few years, when those realities felt especially acute.

As I prepared to leave after thanking the event organizers for inviting me, a young woman from the group of high schoolers walked up and introduced herself. She told me she was really moved by my story about Mercy Project and handed me a 20-dollar donation. I was so moved by her act of generosity that I gave my own 20 dollars to Mercy Project and pinned hers to the bulletin board in my office to remind me that we should always strive to give what we have and not what we have left.

> We should always strive to give what we have and not what we have left.

Two years later, a young woman came up to me after my first lecture of the semester at Texas A&M. "I don't know if you remember me," she said, "but we met two years ago when you spoke to my group just before I started college. I've wanted to take your class ever since I heard you speak that day."

I immediately remembered her. "You forgot the most important part," I said. "The 20 dollars you generously donated that day." She smiled bashfully, and I continued. "I'm going to show you a picture next week that I think you'll appreciate."

The next week after class, I showed her the picture of her 20-dollar bill still hanging on my bulletin board and told her the story of how inspiring her gift had been for me. It was clear she was moved to see the impact her gift had made.

Fast-forward to the present. This young woman graduated with a business degree just as I was writing the final chapters of this book. She is now headed off to a great job in which she will undoubtedly excel. As a graduation gift, I mailed her the 20-dollar bill back, 4 years after she'd first given it to me. I included a note that said, "Keep this somewhere that will help you remember to never lose the heart of that 18-year-old girl about to start college."

Her act of pure compassion was the first domino. That domino nudged me to act in compassion and give to others, who gave to others, who will give to others, and so on. Where it ends, no one knows. But we know where it started. And we all have something of value we can give away. When it comes to money, and almost everything else in life, the amount given away is almost always secondary to the intention. This is what makes just 14 minutes a day of good so compelling.

The full power of good is almost never experienced at the moment it happens. It lives on through the person we showed compassion toward, who will then show it to the next person, and on and on it will go well beyond our original act. We know this is true because we've experienced it in our own lives through people who have shown kindness and compassion toward us in such a way that we want to carry that forth to the next person.

> The full power of good is almost never experienced at the moment it happens.

It's the phenomenon of people going through a drive-thru and paying for the order of the person behind them. This single act of good typically costing just 5 or 10 dollars often has a chain effect that can spontaneously last for hours. All those other people in the drive-thru had no intention of paying for someone else's food that day. But everything changed when someone first paid for theirs. They were shown compassion, they were the recipient of someone else's good, and so they choose to show it as well. At some point, someone comes along and that specific chain breaks for one reason or another, but not before it has made a significant impact, the tail of which we may never know.

> Compassion begets compassion and good
> begets good because both give us permission to
> unleash creativity, imagination, and kindness.

How many of the people who benefitted from the domino effect of good are more likely to be the ones to start it the next time? Almost all of them. They benefitted from the falling of the first domino, which helped them believe they could now be the first domino themselves. Compassion begets compassion and good begets good because both give us permission to unleash creativity, imagination, and kindness. An act of good from someone else shakes us out of our "all about me" bubble and reminds us of all the people we engage every day who need to be seen and loved in the ways we all wish we were seen and loved.

Not every act of compassion turns into some huge domino effect. But sometimes, every once in a while, we do something good, kind, and compassionate that leads to the most unexpected chain of events.

Consider the story of a woman named Miranda. A few years ago, Miranda sent me a Facebook message. She told me that several years earlier, she'd read a post I had written that had been shared by one of her friends. She included a link to the original post as well. It wasn't one that had gone viral or even been overwhelmingly well received. It was just an "okay" post from years before—one I had honestly kind of forgotten I'd ever written until I received this random message.

Something about my words in that original post had spoken to what she had been feeling in that specific season of her life. Miranda and her husband are singers/songwriters from Austin, Texas, and she immediately sat down after reading the post and started writing a song inspired partly by the words I'd shared. That beautiful song, called "Promised Land," was released in 2018, and they chose that song to open each performance of their next tour. Miranda went on to tell me that after every show, people would come up and tell them how that song has changed them for the better and helped them think more about what it means to be fully human. Wow!

Additionally, the seed of that song and what it did inside Miranda led her to create Song Healing classes, where she teaches people (including children in juvenile detention centers) how to use the power of song to process their feelings and emotions.

When Miranda wrote to me, it was to share their song and thank me for the inspiration. She told me she honestly had kind of forgotten how impactful my post had been until it popped up in her Facebook memories the week before.

Can you see the domino effect?

- A guy on the internet uses words of good to share his heart for unity with others.
- Someone shares the post.
- A stranger reads it.
- The stranger is a talented musician who writes a song inspired partly by how those words made her feel.
- She sings that song to audiences across the country.
- It helps those people feel new things.
- She also uses the gift of songwriting to help others write songs.
- That helps those people feel new things and begin healing from their trauma.
- And what will those people do now?

This is the power of the domino effect of good. 'Round and 'round and 'round it goes.

By the way, the Facebook post that originally inspired Miranda was the one you read in the last chapter about the two people sitting across a table from each other and just holding hands and feeling the weight of their shared humanity. One of the stanzas in her song goes like this:

Will you reach for my hand?
Take me to your promised land
If I'm standing all alone.

Will you say my name?
Even if we don't look the same
Will you see my face in your own?

These are the questions that a billion hours of good asks us every day. May we say "yes" and trust that our simple "yes" might just stretch farther and deeper and wider than we could ever imagine.

Now that we've uncovered just a few of the myriad opportunities we have every day to look within ourselves for compassion as we respond to the world around us with good, it's time to move to what keeps us from doing more of these good things in the first place. So many of us want to *do more good*, but there's something (or several things) holding us back. Even if we agree that we need less time and money than we first believed necessary to drive positive change, how do we overcome our fears of actually doing something? Where do we find the courage to be the kind of people who confidently go out and create the good we know the world so desperately needs? These are the exact questions that the next six chapters answer. And it all starts with finding our North Star.

> Where do we find the courage to be the kind of people who confidently go out and create the good we know the world so desperately needs?

## Reflections on Compassion

1. Can you remember a time when you felt compassion all the way down in your gut?
2. How do you tend to respond to this type of compassion?
3. Do you find it easy or difficult to see the people you encounter every day as your neighbors?
4. Do you believe words create worlds? If not, why? If so, do you treat words as such?
5. Can you remember a time someone used words to help bring you healing or peace?
6. How did you feel when you read the chapter about the "other"?
7. Who are some of the "others" in your life?
8. Would you say you are a friend "to" or "with" the "others" in your life?
9. Is your tendency to put up walls or pull up more chairs? Why?
10. What scares you the most about inviting more people to your table?
11. Can you recall a time you were personally impacted by the domino effect of good?
12. What scares you the most about being this first domino to fall?
13. Do you believe compassion is a muscle that grows larger when it's used more?

# CHAPTER TEN

# Our
# North Star

If we're honest, many of us are not who we always hoped we would be. As children, we dared to dream audacious dreams. We wanted to accomplish big, bold, beautiful things, and we promised ourselves we'd do whatever it took to meet those goals in life. We even shared those plans with others, with no fear of anyone thinking less of us. The world was ours!

In those days, we'd look up at the stars and truly believe we would touch them. And then, well, life happened.

Some of those changes are just a natural part of growing older, becoming more responsible and embracing all the constraints (real or perceived) that adulthood entails. But somewhere along the way, many of us lost the courage to chase our dreams. And I'm not talking about our dream job—it's more than that. We lost that sense of wanting to give our lives to our biggest, boldest, and most beautiful goals. We lost the courage to both dream big and reach for those stars. In ways big and small, this affects our ability to do good in the world because many of us are no longer sure we can actually make the difference we once believed we could. We doubt our ability to make a profound impact, and so we do nothing at all.

> It's not too late for us to find our courage again.
> In fact, it's imperative if we want to reach our
> goal of a billion hours of good together.

I have good news for us today. Incredible news, actually. It's not too late for us to find our courage again. In fact, it's imperative if we want to reach our goal of a billion hours of good together.

Let me explain by telling you the story of my dear friend Fuseini.

Fuseini was born in 1989 in a very small, rural community in Ghana, Africa. His mother never attended a day of school, and his father only completed kindergarten. Both his parents worked as farmers on a very small plot of land near their one-room family home. Money was always tight, but Fuseini's mom made it a priority for her children to attend school, and so they did.

It wasn't easy, but Fuseini's mother somehow kept stretching the family's finances, and those kids honored her commitment by continuing to show up and work hard every day in their rural school, where the room held far more children than desks. As Fuseini neared the end of high school in 2009 (a huge feat in and of itself for someone from his community), he took the required exams to attend college. Studying at a university had always been a dream of his. Unfortunately, he was not accepted into a single college program. Upon receiving this difficult news, he "lost his courage," as he so poignantly described to me one day. Soon after, he returned home to work on his family farm, and it seemed his fate in life was sealed.

A few years later, Fuseini learned that someone a few miles down the road was seeking day laborers for a construction project. The project was being funded by the nonprofit mission Stacey and

I had recently started—Mercy Project. The building would provide our team in Ghana with a place to live. When Fuseini heard about this rare opportunity, he showed up to apply for a job. He was hired by our Ghanaian general contractor and soon began working through long, hot days, making bricks for the house. The going rate for an inexperienced day laborer was not much, but it was a job and he was grateful. Fuseini would work all day and then ride his old bicycle several miles home, where he'd work again until dark on the family farm. He did this every day for almost a year. At the end of the year, he was the last worker left on the job site. Others had quit, been fired, or simply drifted off. Fuseini outworked them all, with his trademark smile on his face.

One of our original team members saw him in those last months of construction and couldn't help but notice his incredible work ethic. So Mercy Project hired Fuseini to be our security guard once construction of the house was complete. He would farm all day and then come spend the night as a watchman, ensuring our team was safe while they slept. As our trust in him grew, so did both his daily responsibilities and salary. He was eventually managing the entire house, including tending the grounds, overseeing all repairs, and generally just making sure everything that needed to be done got done. He quickly become our go-to guy, and we all recognized his many contributions.

At the end of 2019, Fuseini was hired as a full time fieldworker for Mercy Project, a promotion that was probably overdue. In this role, he's become the first employee to fill this position without a college degree, but he's now handling significant leadership responsibilities as our organization continues rescuing and reintegrating trafficked children back into their family units. But that's not all. Fuseini recently told me that his work with Mercy Project, as well as his relationships with our American staff living in Ghana, have helped him to "find his courage" once again. He proved his point by pulling out a letter of acceptance for a Ghanaian university. He'd already started taking night and weekend classes to earn that coveted degree. As he shared his good news, I'm not sure which one of us had the bigger smile.

It took Fuseini nearly a decade of patience and a ton of hard work, but he finally found his courage again. You can too. And it doesn't have to take 10 years or involve the task of making bricks by hand under the hot African sun. It's a decision you can and should start making today.

> Finding our courage means we remember who and what we wanted to be before something set us off course.

Finding our courage means we remember who and what we wanted to be before something set us off course. It requires us to step back and take honest inventory of our current life situation, asking,

- Am I who I want and need to be?
- Am I doing what I want and need to be doing with my time and energy?
- If this were the end of my life, would I be satisfied with what I've poured myself into and the impact I've made in other lives?

Do those questions seem impractical or unrealistic? I can hear some of you saying, "Ha! It must be nice to be able to ask those questions!" If that's what you're thinking, then I want to challenge you to ask yourself what it is about them that scares you so much. Because the first act of finding our courage again might be to stop making excuses about who is really in control of our lives.

I believe we've each been given a North Star, a steady guide that keeps us moving in the right direction even when life gets hard or confusing. Knowing how to find our North Star helps ensure we're actually going where we want to be going. That seems important, doesn't it? Asking "Am I who I want to be?" and "Am I doing what I want to be doing?" are much more easily answered when we can look toward our North Star to lead the way.

When we know where we want to go, we can no longer lie to ourselves about whether or not we're actually headed there. Because, trust me, we're all really good at lying to ourselves.

The importance of the astronomical North Star is historically long and fascinating. But the most well-known more modern connection is associated with that of the Underground Railroad during the dark period of slavery in our nation. At a time when slaves in the South were trying to escape to freedom in the North, Harriet Tubman and many other incredibly brave and heroic freedom fighters would encourage those fleeing for their lives to use the North Star to guide them through the safest route. Maps and compasses were rare, so this North Star was everything. As the consequences of death and severe physical punishment loomed large over their perilous journey, escaping slaves used this star as a lifeline through the most dire and dangerous circumstances.

I don't use this analogy lightly or take it for granted when I encourage you to find your North Star. Many of us don't know where we're heading in life. We've lost sight of our North Star and are no longer moving toward our most meaningful goals and dreams. Others may claim to be following their North Star, but only in word and rarely in deed.

Not sure what direction you're heading? Unable to identify your North Star? Take a look at your calendar, budget, and credit card statements. Where do you invest the bulk of your time and resources? In what direction is most of your energy flowing?

As uncomfortable as it might be, this quick and objective assessment can offer a clear indicator of what you value most at this stage in your life. These two questions will reveal your true North Star. Then the question becomes: Is this the North Star you want to follow? Or do you need to reset your compass for a truer north? These are the questions we should seek to answer throughout both the next chapters and the rest of our lives.

Since 2015, I've had the privilege of teaching an undergraduate business class in the Mays Business School at Texas A&M University. It's one of the best business schools in America, and every semester I am blown away by the quality of the young people who sit in my classroom. The specific course I teach is called "Business Solutions to Social Problems," and one of the distinct highlights for me as a lecturer is learning with and from the amazing young people who sign up to take the class. Every semester, I use my opening class session to introduce myself, share my North Star, and ask the students to consider theirs. The end of that lecture culminates in their first homework assignment of the semester: "Write a journal entry that tells me about your North Star. Equally important, tell me whether or not you are pursuing this North Star with the passion and energy a true North Star deserves."

Reading the journal entries that first week is always a treat. For one, it's a gift to get to know my students better by having them share some of their most significant values, but there's more to it than that, as student after student realizes they haven't been giving their North Star the attention it deserves. Somewhere along the way, in the chaos of deadlines and tests and internships and social connections, many of them have forgotten what mattered most to them.

I am empathetic to my students' reflections, because they are my reflections too. You might find that you also relate to their struggle. But I'm here to tell you it's never too late to rediscover our North Star and to reignite the courage within us so we can follow that route to a more meaningful life. I know this in part because my students submit a reflection journal at the end of every semester and more than a few of them, for more than 12 semesters in a row now, have written that reidentifying their North Star at the beginning of the semester led to significant changes in their behaviors, habits, and actions. That story can be your story as well, and I hope it will be.

> I'm here to tell you it's never too late to rediscover our North Star and to reignite the courage within us so we can follow that route to a more meaningful life.

Eric Roth, an American screenwriter of landmark films, including *Forrest Gump*, *The Curious Case of Benjamin Button*, and *A Star Is Born*, says it in a way that really resonates with me: "It's never too late or, in my case, too early to be whoever you want to be. . . . I hope you feel things you never felt before. I hope you meet people with a different point of view. I hope you live a life you're proud of. If you find that you're not, *I hope you have the courage to start all over again*" (emphasis mine).

Finding our courage means being willing to ask ourselves if we are living a life we're proud of. It's looking in the mirror past the extra 10 pounds and the wrinkles and the gray hair (or, in my case, the lack of hair) and saying, "I only get one shot at this, and I want to make the greatest impact possible in every way I can."

This is a critical step in our commitment to being a part of the billion hours of good movement. We must choose—and, yes, it is a choice—that we want to spend our lives making the most significant impact possible and adjust our course when we realize we haven't been following our North Star.

Finding our courage means making the conscious decision to be all in. It's recognizing that where we find ourselves is where we chose to be, not where someone else or our culture or past life experiences told us to be. It's not a one-time permanent choice we make, but a daily one, to follow our North Star the best we can wherever we are and with whatever we have. It's a beautiful way to live life.

Finding our courage means we follow our North Star instead of running away from it. It means we daily creep up to the edge of the diving board, look down into the water, and then leap off— even if we're afraid (with bonus points for cannonballs). It means we say "yes" to the opportunities that make us feel most alive, and we make space for the moments that stir our soul.

> Finding our courage means we follow our North Star instead of running away from it.

Finding our courage means we adopt and embrace a new battle cry and mantra: "Why not me? Why not now?"

We all know courage when we see it, even from a very young age. My daughter Micah was eight years old when her great uncle Alan was admitted back into the hospital for the cancer that would ultimately end his life a few months later. Micah is a deep feeler and encourager who loves making elaborate handmade cards for people. But this time, the artwork on her card was simple and the words profound and direct: "I'm sorry you're back in the hospital. You're very brave."

Uncle Alan was brave. Micah could see that, without anyone having to tell her. Her pure heart wanted to tell him exactly what she saw, and so she did. I love that about kids.

If Micah could make a card for each of you reading this book, she would say you are brave too. Because you are. Brave enough to want to do more good. Brave enough to open this book. Brave enough to let yourself feel more compassion toward others. Brave enough to find your courage again and reclaim your true North Star. Brave enough to start living out those big dreams and bold ideas that you buried in a box under your backyard treehouse long ago. Brave enough to make the conscious decision that you have spent your last day waiting for everyone else to tell you how you should think or feel or live. Choosing to live out a billion hours of good compels us to find our North Star. But that is just the beginning of our journey to find our courage and make the greatest possible impact on the world. Courage also means so much more:

- Courage is showing up.
- Courage is choosing hard things.
- Courage is failing and getting back up.
- Courage is telling the truth.
- Courage is saying, "I'm sorry."

These are the exact ideas we'll walk through in the next five chapters as we find our courage again—together.

# CHAPTER ELEVEN

# It Starts with Showing Up

In 2019, Mike, a senior at Texas A&M, asked me if I'd be his mentor. I'd met this young man two times, but he'd never been a student of mine and we didn't have any formal relationship. Although flattered by his interest in learning from me, I was honest in telling him that I had very little extra time at that moment. Sensing his disappointment, I offered to meet with him once but was clear it would be nearly impossible to commit to anything ongoing. Just to make sure he didn't feel like I was blowing him off, I tagged on one final option: "Mike, I don't know how you feel about running, but six days a week, I start my day with a run through my neighborhood. If you're willing to drive to my house and run with me at 5:30 in the morning, we could use that time to learn together as often as you'd like."

Without even the slightest hesitation, he agreed, but I never expected him to show up on my front porch just a few days later.

It was raining and freezing cold the morning Mike arrived in the dark, running shoes on his feet. A big storm kept us from hitting the roads together that morning, but we sat on the front porch, surrounded by an impressive show of lightning and thunder, and visited anyway.

We've run together a number of times over the last year, which has allowed us to form a true mentor–mentee relationship. More than that, Mike has become my friend. I was even given the honor of officiating his marriage to his beautiful bride, Mallory.

How did this kind of trusting relationship develop between two strangers? It happened because Mike dared to show up—and in doing so, he opened himself up to opportunities that never would have existed otherwise. He certainly could have come once, run with me, asked me a few questions, and then been on his way. But then he would have missed out on the prospect of gaining the trust, mentorship, and friendship of someone he wanted to learn from. So he chose to bravely take the risk of showing up. And now we're both better for it.

> Getting out of bed, lacing up our shoes, opening the front door, and putting our hearts into the world with no idea how they will be handled—these are our first steps along our journey to courage.

Mike seemed to intuitively understand that true courage begins with having the guts to show up. Getting out of bed, lacing up our shoes, opening the front door, and putting our hearts into the world with no idea how they will be handled—these are our first steps along our journey to courage.

How many opportunities have we missed because we never dared to show up? New relationships, new jobs, new foods, new books, new movies, new ideas, new chances to do good and make the world a better place—the list could go on and on. Have you ever attended an event that you really didn't feel like attending?

And have you ever reached the end of the night and found yourself thinking, *I'm so glad I came?*

That's the power of showing up.

Now I know the introverts (Hi to my lovely wife—I love you!) are thinking, *Hey, I experience plenty of growth right here with a good book and a tall glass of wine.* I won't deny that growth and a general recharging can certainly happen in a quiet spot in a favorite room of your house. But at some point, we have to venture outside our favorite reading nook in order for much of our growth journey to happen. There's just no way around it. Eventually we all have to make the intentional decision to change out of our PJs, comb our hair, and go. And when we go, we grow.

I'm not suggesting we all live some sort of fairytale, utopian life where every new experience and opportunity suddenly becomes life changing in the best way possible. We all know this is not the case. Much of the challenge of showing up is that the vast majority of the time, nothing extraordinary at all will happen. But to paraphrase an old quote, showing up will give us two consistent options: every time we show up, we can either succeed or learn.

When we succeed, something great will result. But when we learn, something great happens too. Or as Wayne Gretzky once said (and Michael Scott from *The Office* famously borrowed later): "We miss 100 percent of the shots we do not take." I also want to note what my friend Terry Howell pointed out when we first discussed the "succeed or learn" concept: "If we're intentional, we can both succeed and learn."

There are certainly moments when we know something has the chance to become a transformative event in our lives. But those moments are rare. Most of the great successes come to us in the ordinary and mundane situations, when no one else is looking. Even these can occur only if we first show up to meet them.

Everyone would choose to show up to accept the Super Bowl trophy, for example. Millions have dreamed of that confetti-filled moment of fortune and fame. But how many actually show up for the years and years of workouts, injuries, rehab sessions, meticulous dieting, and late nights studying plays and watching films to perfect their skills? Courage and transformation appear in the thousands of mundane and ordinary moments, not the few moments when the cameras are rolling and everyone is cheering. But those stellar athletes would never have reached that moment of cameras and cheering without first having the courage to show up decades earlier, with no fanfare, with no one paying attention, and with no guarantee of success. The same is true for us.

> If I look back at some of the most extraordinary and meaningful moments of my life, the majority are marked with one common thread that runs through them: I made a conscious decision to show up.

If I look back at some of the most extraordinary and meaningful moments of my life, the majority are marked with one common thread that runs through them: I made a conscious decision to show up. I did not know what these situations might lead to or if they would lead to anything at all, but I chose to show up anyway. Here are just a few examples from my own life:

- At 19 years old, I read a newspaper article listing the current mayoral candidates in my hometown and decided I too would run for mayor. I showed up, signed up, and ended up placing third out of five candidates. I did not win that election, but that moment changed me forever (and makes for one heck of a party story). It started with showing up.

- Also at 19, I ran my first 26.2-mile marathon—completely untrained. If that sounds awful, it's because it absolutely was. I was chasing a girl I liked and planned to run just a few miles with her. I ended up running the entire stupid, painful, blood-inducing marathon. Now I've run 26 marathons (placing in the top 5 percent in my last one), and I actively coach several other runners in their marathon training. I did not win that first marathon (nor did I win the girl!), but I showed up. Not only did that experience turn me into a lifelong runner, but it also led to my launching an annual marathon in my hometown that has now seen more than 20,000 people cross its finish line and raised more than a million dollars for local children's charities. It started with showing up.

- In 2009, I read the previously mentioned book about child trafficking in Ghana, Africa. I was absolutely shocked to learn of this reality and felt compelled to help. I Googled the author's name, contacted her, and a few months later got off a plane with her in Ghana. Within a year, I'd quit my job and founded an anti-human-trafficking nonprofit that has grown into an internationally recognized and award-winning organization. We've since rescued more than 180 children out of human trafficking and returned them to their families. I did not plan to start this organization when I called the author. But I showed up. First to call her. Then to go to Africa with her. Then to quit my job. I showed up thousands of days in a row and asked others to show up with me, and when I did so, something extraordinary happened. It all started with showing up.

I could tell you a hundred more stories from my life about the power of showing up. But here's the important takeaway: Showing up is not some extraordinary talent or gift that only I possess. That's the power of it. Showing up requires absolutely zero talent or skills. In the last example I listed, that author's incredible book was actually a *New York Times* best seller, read by tens of thousands of people, including Oprah Winfrey. I do not know how many of those readers called and asked to go to Africa with the author, but I would assume not very many. And did anyone else subsequently quit their job to respond to the crisis in the best way they could? Unlikely. I was not any more capable or qualified than anyone else who read that book. I was only 27 years old and had no experience with human trafficking at all. But I followed my heart and dared to show up.

Courage is having a willingness to put yourself out there with no guarantee of what will come next. Some of those times will result in failure (more on that soon), but we'll never know when we will fail and when we will succeed unless we actually show up in the first place. Every significant event in the history of the world started because someone showed up—even though they did not know what the outcome would be.

> Courage is having a willingness to put yourself out there with no guarantee of what will come next.

So what is it that keeps us from showing up? This is the question we have to answer before we can move on. Because it's one thing for me to say, "Hey, courage means showing up. So show up!" But it's something else for you to make the intentional decision to start showing up in your own life. If we're truly going to show up 14 minutes at a time, day after day, we have to start by being forthright about what keeps us from showing up in the first place. The breakthrough comes when we learn to be honest with ourselves about why showing up scares us so darn much.

If I polled a large group of diverse people on why they personally choose not to show up to try new and different things, I would certainly get a smattering of answers. Some would seem very practical ("I'm too busy"), some would seem reflective ("I don't know how to do that thing"), but only a few would be honest enough to say, "I choose not to show up because I am scared to fail or be rejected."

At the very root of it, our unwillingness to show up comes from a fear of failing. I know this for several reasons.

One reason is because I commonly ask people this question and keep asking them until we get to the root of their reluctance. When people who trust me are pressed, they will often readily admit that they would rather fail at showing up in the first place than show up and fail. The difference? Control.

We feel like we are in full control when we choose not to show up. We keep the "power." But we concede that power to a million other factors when we show up without certainty about what will happen next. And that reality alone is enough to scare many of us into never showing up at all. To quote the marvelous Brené Brown (whom I have a lifetime goal of hanging out with one day): "The courage to be vulnerable is not about winning or losing; it's about the courage to show up when you can't predict or control the outcome."

Another reason I know this to be true is because the most highlighted line in the Kindle version of my first book, *Disrupting for Good*, reads: "My life was changed forever when my willingness to dream and take chances outgrew my fear of failure." I thought very little of that line when I wrote it, but it is the line that resonated most deeply with the largest number of my readers. That is not an accident. We all desire to outgrow our fear of failure.

> If you're reading this book and you're afraid of failing, I want you to hear me say I see you because I *am* you.

I know for a fact that we often do not show up out of a fear of failure because I still, at times, make the choice not to show up for the very same reason. I understand this line of thinking because it is often my line too. So if you're reading this book and you're afraid of failing, I want you to hear me say I see you because I *am* you. The spot next to you on that comfortable, safe couch is mine, and it is just as worn and tattered as the place in which you sit.

I get it. But because I get it, I am not going to let us stay here. Staying here will come at an enormous cost that we cannot even measure because we do not know what we will miss out on and, by proxy, what the rest of the world will miss out on too.

Our world is so beautifully interconnected that I might miss out on an opportunity because you choose not to show up and vice versa. This statement isn't intended to instill some sort of guilt or shame, but instead to emphasize that we are all threaded together in lovely and complicated ways, and we are so much better when we share this journey with one another. In other words, my life will be made better by your courage to show up. After all:

- I can never see the painting you do not paint.
- I can never hear the song you do not sing.
- I can never try the food you do not cook.
- I can never read the book you do not write.
- I can never laugh at the joke you do not tell.
- Most importantly, there are people, causes, movements, problems that will never be helped, uplifted, empowered, and made right if you are too scared to show up.

When we choose not to show up, we deprive both ourselves and the others around us of something delightful—our incredible presence.

As Glennon Doyle says, "If you feel something calling you to dance or write or paint or sing, please refuse to worry about whether you're good enough. Just do it. Be generous. Offer a gift to the world that no one else can offer: yourself."

Is that not a lovely thought? Each one of us can offer the world a uniquely magnificent gift—ourselves. It costs us no money, and we can come as we are. So let's be people who choose to have the courage to show up. Let's make this choice not just for ourselves but for one another. Let's be brave!

# CHAPTER TWELVE

# *Für Elise* and Hospital Chaplaincy

If we're going to change the world, even 14 minutes at a time, it's going to be hard sometimes. So let me start with the bad news: we stink at doing hard stuff. Now the good news: it does not have to stay this way.

So many of our daily routines have been created with one singular goal in mind: comfort. We set our clocks with soothing alarms so as not to startle us awake too suddenly. We slip into our plush house shoes the moment we get home. We use an electronic toothbrush and razor, shower with perfectly warmed water, press a button to start our freshly brewed coffee—you get the point. I could list many experiences that give us great comfort. Who doesn't like comfort?

But all this comfort comes at a cost. Because what is the opposite of comfort? Discomfort. And what happens when an entire culture is set up around keeping people from experiencing discomfort and pain? We become both shockingly unprepared for it and awful at responding when it does invariably come.

Corporate America calls this soft skill of being able to respond to challenges *resilience* or *grit*, and they are desperate to find it in the employees they are hiring to work for them. This is new, by the way. Companies have not always had to figure out if a prospective employee had grit or resilience because it used to be assumed that all of them did. In a modern world full of unprecedented comforts, that is changing.

Google has this really fascinating tool called Google Trends. It allows you to go as far back as 2004 (when they started tracking data) to see the relative popularity of a word based on how many times people searched for it. Take for example the word *resilience*. The word *resilience* is currently typed into Google and searched at a rate five times as often as it was just 16 years ago. It seems many of us are searching for something we didn't know we'd need.[1]

> The word *resilience* is currently typed into Google and searched at a rate five times as often as it was just 16 years ago. It seems many of us are searching for something we didn't know we'd need.

The generations before us did not need to search the internet to understand resilience because it woke them up by way of roosters in the morning and followed them all the way to bed late at night when their chores were done. They did not need books on the topic because they were living the story. My grandmother grew up on a farm in Waco, Texas, in the 1940s. Her parents worked very hard to give her an easier childhood than they had, but even as a young girl, she "kept weights" for her dad in the cotton fields, watched her brother and sister bale hay, and once worked alongside a friend for days to earn three dollars each for handpicking three acres of cotton. Her mom sewed most of their clothes, they went barefoot most of the time at home, and if they wanted fried chicken, then "Mother had to chase down a chicken and go through multiple steps to prepare it for frying." My grand-mother was neither poor nor rich. But she was resilient. Like most everyone else she knew. She did not have to choose to do hard things, because her life naturally included hard things already. But this allowed her to become resilient and full of grit and willing to work hard. She did not view her life as difficult or unfair because it was just the life she had. Even though she is now well into her eighties and has many of the comforts I mentioned before, she has never forgotten those days of growing up on a farm as a young girl and the ways it shaped and formed her, even to this day. She is not scared of pain or discomfort because she's already experienced a whole lot of it and has lived to talk about it. Like nearly everyone else who grew up in her generation of Americans, she's got grit.

But the world today is not the same as it used to be. Now there are entire industries, massive ones, built around making our lives more pleasant and comfortable. The problem is not the comforts, but the way these comforts have shielded us from experiencing discomfort. Doing so has come at a significant cost. No spa or mocha cappuccino or smartphone can keep us from the truth that life will sometimes be hard. And when we rarely experience hard situations or challenges, we're more likely to crumble when they do come.

> No spa or mocha cappuccino or smartphone can keep us from the truth that life will sometimes be hard.

There is a new term I have heard people use for parents who protect their children from challenges and difficulty. People used to call these "helicopter parents" because they were always hovering over their children, making sure nothing went wrong; but now I hear the term "lawnmower parents."[2] This refers to parents who go out in front to cut down all the tall weeds, and scare away all the snakes, and ensure the path is smooth before their children follow behind them. The irony in this illustration is that the child, of course, has no idea that any of this has been done for them. They walk the path under the impression that this is how life is for everyone because this is how life has always been for them. And many of us are not all that different from the children in this illustration, enjoying our relatively obstacle-free journeys with the expectation that this is how life will always be. This becomes a big problem when there is no longer anything to protect us from what is ahead, which makes it all the more important that we have the courage to do hard things (with intention).

One time I started writing a new book, with the working title *It's Good to Do Hard Things: What I Learned from Doing One Hard Thing Every Day for a Year.* Well, it turns out that doing a hard thing every day is . . . really hard. I did great for the first month, even the first six weeks. There were certainly a few "Oh no, it's 9:00 p.m. and I forgot to do something hard today!" moments in there; but for the most part, it went well. Until it didn't. But even in spite of my failure on that book (more on failure in the next chapter—I have plenty of those stories to share with you), my hypothesis remains the same. To get better at doing hard things, we have to *do more hard things*!

> To get better at doing hard things, we
> have to *do more hard things*!

Courage is choosing to do those hard things. On purpose. Because those hard things are how the world is changed. Because those hard things are how we are changed. Because those hard things are where real transformation takes place. Because those hard things are how a bunch of ordinary people will join together to create a billion hours of good. And because, at some point, hard things will come that we did not choose, and how we respond will be directly tied to all the times we have previously chosen to do hard things on purpose.

We often do not attempt hard things for the same reason we often choose not to show up: It is scary and uncomfortable, and we are afraid of failing. Believing we are incapable gives us a built-in excuse. That self-limiting belief is a metaphorical mattress we drag with us everywhere we go so we'll have a soft place to land when things get even the slightest bit difficult. The truth is that we are indeed capable. But are we willing? That is the one honest question many of us will spend an entire lifetime trying to avoid.

> What we must reckon with is that in being unwilling to try hard things, we are almost certainly ensuring we will fail when the unexpected hard things of life come— and they will absolutely come, whether we like it or not.

What we must reckon with is that in being unwilling to try hard things, we are almost certainly ensuring we will fail when the unexpected hard things of life come—and they will absolutely come, whether we like it or not.

A young woman in my business class at Texas A&M wrote these poignant words several years ago in her reflection journal, and they moved me so much that I saved them. Here is what she said:

> I do not know when I became afraid of doing hard things. I do not know how I lost that part of myself. I used to call the White House when I was little because I had questions. Now I barely go to my professor's office hours. The lesson I am learning is when you see a need, fill that need. Act on what you believe. Recently, I sent an email that was inspired by this class. "I have an idea that I would really like to run by you. I don't know if

it has been done before. Would it be possible to get 20 minutes of your time to talk about it?"

I sent an email and things are happening. I am still scared of failing. I am still scared of doing hard things. BUT I am thinking about the hard things that need to be done, which is a good step. (Quoted here with permission from my former student.)

My goal as a teacher is to get my students to start thinking about those hard things that need to be done. Those hard things we can choose because we know they are going to make us better. Those hard things that are the only way for us to experience true transformation. Those hard things that will first change us and then change the world around us.

I want to share with you a few hard and uncomfortable things I have chosen to do in my life—choices that have made me a better husband, father, son, friend, and human being.

One of them is being a volunteer chaplain. The main problem with volunteering for this position is that sometimes people actually need you—people who are facing tremendous pain.

I was called to the hospital one day because the regular chaplain was out of town. I'd been on call before, but I'd never been needed. But that day a father was dying, and the family wanted someone to pray with them. That's all I knew when I walked into the hospital room.

Their father had taken his last breath, surrounded by his family, just seconds before I'd walked in. They were heartbroken. Weeping, they held his hand, stroked his cheek, and hugged him. They said good-bye as only the truly hurting can do. It was both beautiful and painful to witness. They hardly even noticed me for a few moments until, all of a sudden, they did.

At first, I just nodded and said nothing. There was nothing to say. Then they asked me when his body would get cold and when the staff would come to take him away. I couldn't answer those questions with certainty. I didn't pretend to know the answers. Then they asked me questions about his soul, about heaven, and about how long it took for him to be with God. I couldn't answer those questions with certainty either. But I stood there with them in their pain, which was one of the most difficult and uncomfortable and beautiful things I've ever done. And. It. Was. Hard.

Then they asked me to pray. It was a muddled prayer. Pitiful really. But they couldn't even hear me—they were sobbing too loudly. The actual words didn't matter to them anyway. They just wanted someone to say it was going to be okay. In the moment, they surely felt that nothing would ever be the same again. And in many ways, it wouldn't be.

After the prayer, they hugged me. They thanked me. And I hugged and thanked them. Then I left. To this day, I've never crossed paths with them again, and I probably never will. But I never forgot being there with them. And I'm better for having shared that grief with them, even though it was one of the hardest things I've ever done—something I easily could have avoided by not volunteering to be a chaplain. By not showing up.

On a lighter note, I started taking piano lessons for the first time about two years ago. I am, to put it mildly, completely lacking when it comes to musical ability. I'd never studied a day of orchestra or band or choir through my school years. I have to work hard to sing any melody, and I couldn't read a single note of music when I began. This is exactly why I wanted to do this—because I know how important it is to do hard things, especially for rewards that can only unfold slowly over months and months of real effort. Consider it my battle cry against a world of instant gratification.

A BILLION HOURS OF GOOD

So every week this dear, kind, and incredibly patient piano teacher extraordinaire shows up and graciously helps me move just a little further down the road. In between those weekly lessons, I carve out 10 to 15 minutes, 3 to 4 times a week, to practice. I am currently learning *Für Elise* by Beethoven, one of my very favorite songs on the piano. I am, truth be told, butchering it badly right now. But each week it sounds slightly more recognizable. Progress.

I recently turned 38 years old, and my life is full of many good things. Yet I find myself drawn to this simple yet difficult practice of persistence. Creating music, even with notes as herky-jerky as mine, does something *good* for my soul. And I want to always say yes to things that do something good for my soul. Even when they're hard. Maybe especially when they're hard. Because those are the things that change me.

Standing with a family in their darkest hour and sitting down at a piano to learn a new song may seem like they do not have much in common. But they do. They have everything in common for me. They are both uncomfortable, they are both challenging, and they are both hard. And, most importantly, they are both voluntary.

I choose to show up and do these hard things because they make me a better person. It's unlikely that I will ever play a large piano concert in front of many people or be called to the hospital when a celebrity falls ill. But that was never the point. The end goal was to dig deep under the layers of comfortability and discover a version of myself that could not be found without challenge and difficulty. A version of myself that could be found only if I showed up.

As Brené Brown puts it, "We can choose courage or we can choose comfort, but we can't have both. Not at the same time." I want us to choose courage. I want us to choose to do the hard things. On purpose. Maybe not every day, but most days. Because these are the moments in which we are changed, made better, and transformed. By choosing courage and doing hard things, we will start changing the world 14 minutes at a time. It will not always be easy, but it will always be worth it. I promise.

> I want us to choose courage. I want us to choose to do the hard things. On purpose. Maybe not every day, but most days. Because these are the moments in which we are changed, made better, and transformed.

### NOTES

[1] "Resilience," Goggle Trends, accessed November 20, 2020, https://trends.google.com/trends/explore?q=resiliencc&date=all&geo=US.
[2] Nicole Pelletiere, "Move Aside Helicopter Moms, Lawnmower Parents Are on the Rise," *Good Morning America*, September 18, 2018, www.goodmorningamerica.com/family/story/move-helicopter-moms-lawnmower-parents-rise-57805055.

# CHAPTER THIRTEEN

# Failing
# (and Getting
# Back Up Again)

I f we're going to put ourselves out into the world by having the courage to show up, we must accept that sometimes we will fail. This should not surprise nor dissuade us from doing what we know is right.

I've had the interesting experience of having several of my posts on Facebook go "viral," but the one that reached the most people was about failing and getting back up.[1] That particular post was shared almost 100,000 times in just a few days and reached several million people across the world. I wrote that post after Tiger Woods's historic return to win the Masters Tournament in 2019. Here is what I penned that day, just moments after Tiger hugged his family off the eighteenth green at Augusta:

> He had it all. Everything. Until he didn't. And the fall
> was not a small one. It was documented everywhere.
> All his sins, and there were plenty, for the world to see.
> Whispers, finger pointing, head shaking, headlines.

Slowly, with almost nobody watching and even less believing, he started coming back. An injury almost ended the comeback before it even started. He persevered through that as well.

Today, with the world watching, he does it. A generation who years ago sat with their dads watching Tiger win sat with their own kids now and said, "Watch this." A generation inspired to excel at golf by watching Tiger on TV as kids watched one more time today as he passed them on the leaderboard.

His children who watched it all unfold over the last decade with their own parts in the story are waiting for him just off the 18th green. The mom who watched her son have it all, and then lose it all, is waiting too. She never left, by the way. Mommas almost never do.

The story isn't perfect. They never are. We never are. But it's a heck of a good one. Watch closely kids. Being great is one thing. Being great after falling out of grace takes twice as much work and ten times as much courage. That's the good stuff in life. That's why a bunch of old folks got tears in their eyes today.

My words were about the power of failing and getting back up. In retrospect, I should not have been surprised that out of the thousands of thoughts I've posted on social media, it would be these 240 words that would reach the furthest to date. Deep down, we are all drawn to the "hero to villain to hero again" story. I think it is because at our most vulnerable and transparent, we know each one of us is a mix of hero and villain ourselves. So watching someone come back from the bottom to be accepted and forgiven and extended grace, well . . . it gives us all a little hope that maybe we will also be given a second (or a tenth) chance, despite our most glaring missteps.

> Each one of our lives is a series of failures and successes—this reality is not unique to any one of us. What can be unique for each one of us is the amount of grace and compassion we choose to give ourselves and others when we do fail.

The truth we must grapple with in our own quest to do more good is that when we choose to find our courage, show up, and do hard things, we are virtually guaranteeing we will also fail sometimes. There is simply no way around it.

If we never fail, then we are essentially

- not doing hard things,
- not being honest with ourselves about what it means to fail,
- or, most likely, both of the above.

Each one of our lives is a series of failures and successes—this reality is not unique to any one of us. What can be unique for each one of us is the amount of grace and compassion we choose to give ourselves and others when we do fail. What can be unique for each of us is the decision to get up again after those inevitable failures do occur. Because courage is not just showing up; it's also having the audacity to get back up and try again after we've failed. Not once or twice or even 10 times. But over and over again for the rest of our lives.

> Courage is knowing that a conscious decision to show up and do hard things means we are putting ourselves in a position where failure is likely.

Courage is knowing that a conscious decision to show up and do hard things means we are putting ourselves in a position where failure is likely. While no one would choose to experience the pain that failure brings, we cannot allow that potential pain to rob us of the certain growth that occurs when we're willing to attempt the sorts of things that might result in failure.

Any successful person has experienced failure. That's a fact. Those failures rarely make headlines by the time successes have come, but that doesn't mean they never happened. The bigger the dream, the bolder the vision; and the grander the idea, the greater the chance for an enormous flop. It just comes with the territory. If we take risks and put ourselves out there, we will sometimes fail. Here are some of my favorite failing stories from people who failed, got up, and ended up doing pretty okay for themselves in the end. You're likely familiar with a few of these folks:

- J. K. Rowling was a recently divorced single mom living off unemployment. She finally finished the first *Harry Potter* book after five years of hard work and then was rejected by every major publishing house in London—in some cases brutally so.[2]
- Albert Einstein was four years old when he began talking. He didn't get into the college of his choice the first time he applied. He did eventually end up graduating from a university but was employed as a door-to-door insurance salesman long before he was awarded the Nobel Prize in 1921.[3]
- Walt Disney was fired from his job as a reporter with the *Kansas City Star* newspaper for "lacking imagination and having no good ideas." His first business, making animated cartoons, went bankrupt. That same year, he moved to Hollywood and teamed up with his brother to create Disney Brothers Studio, which eventually became the Walt Disney Company. Five years later, he created Mickey Mouse, and the rest is "Take my money!" history.[4]

113

- Vincent Van Gogh spent his short life painting. Sadly, he died by suicide at age 37—nearly the same age I am as I write this. He created more than 2,100 pieces of art in his short life, almost half of which were oil paintings. Before his death, he sold just one of those paintings. One. His entire life was marked by poverty and mental illness, and he considered himself a failure. He never lived to see the positive impact his creations would have on the world, but his legacy speaks for itself.[5]

It's astonishing to consider that people with as much talent and grit as J. K. Rowling, Albert Einstein, Walt Disney, and Vincent Van Gogh all failed, and spectacularly, long before they ever succeeded. But their failures did not mark the end of their stories, and that's why we all know their names today.

How many of us have made the mistake of viewing our previous or current failures as the enduring takeaway of our stories, rather than being just another dot on the plot line of our life? J. K. Rowling could have assumed the odds were also stacked against her. She could have made excuses and claimed she'd never find the time to write as a single mom who needed to "get a real job." Einstein could have spent his entire life telling himself that he was not as smart as everyone else. Walt Disney could have listened to the voices in his head (and outside of it) that said, "You already tried this and failed." And Van Gogh could have stopped painting because, clearly, no one was buying his art. But none of them chose those paths, not permanently at least—and it was a choice! Not a choice they made one time, but over and over again. They chose courage—even when that meant getting back up again after failing. Time and time again.

These stories remain impactful to us today because we know these individuals' names and admire their work. But we should also consider them impactful because they remind us that no one is immune to failing and no one is exempt from facing the hard choices each step of the way. I am here to tell you it is worth it to try, and then to try and try again. You are worth it. The world needs you to get up again after you fail.

I would be remiss to point out the failures of others without talking about some of my own failures too. Failures are not the sort of highlights that make a person's About Me page on their website. I'm betting you might not have even bought this book if the bio on the back read as follows:

> Chris Field has spent a lifetime failing and making a
> fool of himself. From a youth filled with detention and
> teacher conferences, to graduating in the middle of his
> class in high school, to receiving no college scholarships,
> to failing as a pastor, he finally found moderate success
> in a nonprofit he and his wife started. Unfortunately,
> that success was also marked by approximately three
> thousand failures as he muddled his way along, trying
> to figure out what in the world he was doing. He fails
> daily at being a good father and husband and brother
> and son and friend, most notably through his pride and
> impatience. Most of his failures take place in or around
> College Station, Texas, where he lives with his wife and
> four kids.

Some people might buy a book like that because they appreciated the honesty and attempt at humor, but the vast majority of us would smirk and move on. It seems we're more attracted to successful stories because thinking about the failures hits too close to home. But avoiding the truth about failure poses a great risk— the risk of underestimating the number of failures in the lives of others and overestimating the number of failures in our own lives.

> Avoiding the truth about failure poses a great risk—the risk of underestimating the number of failures in the lives of others and overestimating the number of failures in our own lives.

Even with the moderate amount of success I've achieved over the last few years, I do not enjoy talking about my greatest failures. I am uncomfortable with the truth about my mediocre grades in high school, my string of unhealthy dating relationships before I met my wife, my dropping out of law school, my failure to grow the church that hired me as their pastor, and so on.

Here's a story about me that proves how blurry the line between success and failure can be: Less than one year after graduating summa cum laude from college, I was unable to find a job. Unemployed and growing desperate, I was offered a part-time job as a host (they said I was not ready to be a waiter!) at a Chili's Bar and Grill, which I strongly considered taking. At the same time, I was applying for a job as the manager of a Long John Silver's restaurant, even though I had never worked a single day of my life in fast food. It wasn't that I was above taking these jobs, but they certainly weren't my goal after working for years to earn my college degree with honors. This all took place less than four years before I would start the nonprofit that I still run today.

I tell these stories because if all you knew about me was the kind of stuff that makes an author bio or speaker demo reel, you might be inclined to find the various successes I've achieved to be intimidating or out of reach. When that happens (and I do it too when I look at other people), we begin to make internal excuses about how or why someone else has been able to do certain things while we have not. This is so incredibly dangerous and will crush our best dreams before we've even said them aloud. Seeing *only* the success of others is much more likely to make us feel inferior than it is to inspire us to greatness. This is why it is so important for us to understand that each and every person we will ever meet has had some level of failure along the way. Some large, some small, some public, but most private. In fact, if we had to identify a singular common theme running throughout each of our lives, it would be failure. This makes our response to failing all the more important, but it does not make it any easier for us to talk openly about the failures we've each experienced along the way.

> If we had to identify a singular common theme running throughout each of our lives, it would be failure.

During one of my early semesters of teaching at Texas A&M, I was giving a lecture about Mercy Project and why I teach a class called "Using Business to Solve Social Problems." At the end of class, I opened it up for questions. After answering a few easy questions, a young woman raised her hand and bravely said: "It sounds like you've had a good amount of success on many of your ventures. Would you mind telling us about your greatest failure?"

Her question was fantastic. My answer was not. I was not ready to be vulnerable and honest, so I stammered through a pitiful nonanswer worthy of a political press conference. It bugged me for two weeks that I had answered such an important question so poorly. So I ended my next lecture by going back to her poignant question from two weeks prior. I spent a solid 10 minutes talking about some of my biggest failures, both personally and as a leader. This honest vulnerability was not easy, but it was good for my soul.

It took me two tries, but I was able to mostly get it right in the end. That moment stands out to me, though, because my ratio of talking about my successes to my failures is still about 1,000 to 1. Ironically, I would bet the students in my class that semester were more empowered to struggle and fail and get back up again in their own lives because of my transparency about my own failures. They might have been impressed if they had only seen and heard about my successes, but they would have been less likely to believe they could do the same in their own lives.

If our goal is to impress, it makes sense for us to hide our failures. But if our goal is to inspire, then we would do well to talk more openly about the times we failed and chose to get up again. Acknowledging our failures along the way actually makes our successes that much more meaningful.

It is in our failures that we learn the most about life, about ourselves, and about who we do and do not want to be. When we fail, we become better human beings—people more equipped to help those who fail after us.

> If our goal is to impress, it makes sense for us to hide our failures. But if our goal is to inspire, then we would do well to talk more openly about the times we failed and chose to get up again.

The very best teachers I have ever known, both in formal education and outside of it, were not great teachers because the lessons they taught came easily to them. In fact, quite the opposite is true. The best teachers often initially struggle with the subject matter they later teach. It is because of that struggle, not in spite of it, that they became great teachers. They became great teachers because they failed, often many times, before they mastered that skill. Their failures ultimately allowed them to teach from a place of experience rather than theory.

There is great difficulty in teaching, or even appreciating, something that comes easily for us. It is in the struggle of failure that we are able to grow, stretch, and experience real transformation. Our own lives are marked by the kind of growth that can only come from the lived experience of failing yet choosing to get up again.

> It is in the struggle of failure that we are able to grow, stretch, and experience real transformation.

My friend Jeremy is a weight-loss mentor. Jeremy is a great guy, super knowledgeable, funny, and really just the kind of person that makes everyone feel like his friend. But those are not the qualities that make him a successful weight-loss mentor. Jeremy is an astoundingly successful weight-loss mentor because he once lost 200 pounds himself. Yes, 200 pounds! Jeremy teaches and mentors from a place of experience. There was a time in his life, not that many years ago, when he would tell you he was failing at being a physically and emotionally healthy person. During this time, he would turn to food as his crutch. This led to many years of unhappiness and unhealthy weight gain, which culminated in his being kicked off his favorite ride at an amusement park because of his weight. For Jeremy, that was the last straw. He made a commitment to do what he had to do to become the person he knew he wanted to be. That sparked his journey to lose 200 pounds and now mentor others on their journeys of getting back to the version of themselves many have not seen in years.

Jeremy is not a successful weight-loss mentor because he's read countless books on weight loss or obtained a college degree in nutrition. Jeremy is a successful mentor because he teaches from a place of experience. He failed and got back up, many different times, and those failures are what allow him to now help other people experience transformation along with him.

This is the power of using failure as a growth opportunity— our greatest weakness has the potential to become one of our greatest strengths. But failing is only half the battle. We must also choose to get back up and leverage those failures into beautiful new opportunities to choose courage again.

If we're going to dedicate part of our lives to helping others, to creating true transformation, we must understand and accept that failure will come with the territory. But our failures will never define us as long as we are willing to get up again after we fall. Because being great is one thing, but being great after falling from grace takes twice as much work and 10 times as much courage. That's the difference between watching golf on TV and watching your putt fall into the cup on the eighteenth green to win the Master's Tournament.

> This is the power of using failure as a growth opportunity—our greatest weakness has the potential to become one of our greatest strengths.

## NOTES

[1]Chris Field, Facebook post, April 14, 2019, www.facebook.com /christopherfield/posts/10157463317654345.

[2]Jacob Shamsian, "How J. K. Rowling Went from Struggling Single Mom to the World's Most Successful Author, Insider, July 30, 2018, www.insider.com /jk-rowling-harry-potter-author-biography-2017-7.

[3]"Albert Einstein: Fact or Fiction?," History Channel, October 27, 2009, updated June 4, 2020, www.history.com/topics/inventions/einsteins-life-facts -and-fiction.

[4]Alana Horowitz, "15 People Who Were Fired before They Became Filthy Rich: Walt Disney's Newspaper Editor Told the Aspiring Cartoonist He Wasn't Creative Enough," Insider, April 25, 2011, www.businessinsider.com/15-people -who-were-fired-before-they-became-filthy-rich-2011-4#walt-disneys -newspaper-editor-told-the-aspiring-cartoonist-he-wasnt-creative-enough-1.

[5]David Sheward, "7 Facts about Vincent van Gogh," Biography, March 29, 2016, updated June 17, 2020, www.biography.com/news/vincent-van-gogh -biography-facts.

# CHAPTER FOURTEEN

# Slippery
# Watermelons

Every Fourth of July during my childhood, our neighborhood pool would host fun games and contests for all the children and teenagers. It was the only day of the summer they did anything like this, and I remember how much I reveled in the competition and the chance to win. (If you have seen the movie *The Sandlot*, the catcher Ham and I were kindred spirits when it came to the bravado with which we walked past the women—much older than us—lined up in their lounging chairs, covered in tanning oil with enormous sunglasses. My desire to be victorious in these holiday games was as large as my overinflated confidence.)

I can only remember one game clearly, where they would cover a large watermelon in gobs of Vaseline and throw it into the deep end of the pool. The winner of the game would be the person who was able to dive to the bottom and bring that watermelon back to the surface without it slipping out of their hands. It was, if you can imagine, not an easy task for adolescents, and we were quick to lose count of the number of times it squirted out of some-one's arms and back to the bottom of the deep end. But, eventually, someone would manage to grab it, pull it close to their chest, and kick back up to the top of the water, where they then had to heave it out onto the concrete without it slipping away again. No wonder I remember that game—someone is probably still trying to get that same watermelon from the bottom of the pool 25 years later!

> A billion hours of good calls us to be people who embrace the truth regarding first ourselves and then those around us.

I don't know when telling the truth became as slippery as that Vaseline covered watermelon of my youth, but I know it has for many of us. A billion hours of good calls us to be people who embrace the truth regarding first ourselves and then those around us. It requires regular and honest assessments about the realities around us and the ways in which we might make things either better or worse.

Think of the energy we expend trying to chase down the truth today when it used to be so clear. And sometimes it's not us chas-ing the truth but the truth chasing us. "You can't hide from the truth" is a phrase many of us have heard since we were young. "You may be right," many of us whisper back, "but I can spend my entire life trying."

Friends, it does not have to be this way. The truth will indeed set us free. But, first, we must have the courage to find it, own it, and begin telling it.

If you've ever been around a child, then you know how easily the truth comes for children. Of course it does—they're saying it as they see it. No filter. They have yet to become jaded and weary of the truth. They have yet to learn the tiptoe dance of falsehood, projection, and denial. You know that dance, right? It's the one where everybody is thinking the same thing, but no one is going to say it, and we're all just hoping that it goes away or fixes it itself, like the old story of the emperor who has no clothes.

History should teach us that a problem might appear to go away for a time, but it is rarely going to fix itself. Sometimes we find ourselves feeling embarrassed because of the plainness by which children speak the truth as they understand it. But isn't it refreshing to be around a child who is honest? Isn't there something both lovely and freeing about being with people we can fully be our true selves around? These feelings should be the rule and not the rare exception, and they can be if we are willing to embrace the truth. It is long past time that we begin being more honest with ourselves and those around us, because transformation cannot happen outside the truth. I absolutely love the way Jen Hatmaker puts it:

> I cannot say this enough: Truth is on the side of good and right things. It is not to be feared. It is not to be dismissed or suffocated or shoved down. If truth can break a relationship or system or doctrine or identity, that thing was built on a lie. It only had the illusion of stability. Truth can and should be trusted to do what it does, which is set us free. Every lie we tell or protect costs somebody something. Who is paying the bill? Who does that lie serve? Who does that lie keep out or down or broken? It is at the expense of something true and just and whole. . . . I am convinced that lying and pretending and shape-shifting and faking may feel like "keeping the peace" but it will cost you your peace. It is no peace at all.

My response to these words is "Yes, yes, yes, and yes. Let it be so!"

Before I go any further, I need to acknowledge something important. The truth I am referencing here is not the kind of truth that bursts forth when someone has had three too many glasses of whiskey or has gone too many hours in a row without sleep. Telling the truth does not mean we verbalize every single thought that enters into our heads, regardless of the value or pain it might bring to someone else. We all know a truth teller like that in our life, and that is absolutely not what I am suggesting. There is nothing courageous about wielding the truth as a weapon to get us what we want or to push people out of our way. It is possible to be both honest and kind; we are generally just pretty terrible at it. In fact, I would make the case that the vast majority of us are either more prone to honesty (directness) or kindness. It is rare to encounter someone with equal measures of both, but that is what we should each aspire to have.

> It is possible to be both honest and kind; we are generally just pretty terrible at it.

I have long said that we are better off having one friend who loves us enough to tell us the truth than we are to have one hundred friends who tell us what we want to hear. The key phrase in that sentence is "loves us enough" because it implies that my friend loves me at all. We should care enough about the people in our lives that we insist on telling them the truth. We should care enough about the people in our lives that we insist on telling that truth kindly. They should know by our many actions and acts of kindness toward them over the years of our relationship that we truly only want the best for them, even if what we say is hard to hear. This is the sort of truth I'm talking about. A truth that heals wounds instead of creating them. Or, at the very least, a truth that brings along Band-Aids when we know that what we need to say, no matter how kindly we say it, might cause someone pain.

There are two types of truth telling that I want to focus on: internal and external.

Internal truths are the ones we tell ourselves every day: the words that flow through our minds when we wake up, every time we look in the mirror, while we sing in the shower, as we drive to work, as we go about our normal routines, and when we lie in bed trying desperately to fall asleep. These internal truths are critically important because the voices in our heads say much more to us than any voices we encounter outside ourselves.

There is no conclusive data, but a new study suggests that we each have somewhere around 6,200 thoughts every single day.[1] Assuming our minds are thinking the same amount when we are asleep as they are when we are awake, that would be more than 4 thoughts every minute, or more than 1 thought every 15 seconds. All Day. All Night. All. The. Time.

> If we are not extraordinarily careful and self-aware, our own minds can become places where lies become true.

In this context, it is not difficult to see why the internal truths we tell ourselves are so important. All day long, we repeat a story about ourselves in our heads. You're too fat, you're too tall, you're overly confident, you're not smart, you're not [fill in the blank], and on and on. These thoughts go 'round and 'round on an endless loop inside our minds. If we are not extraordinarily careful and self-aware, our own minds can become places where lies become true.

The opposite is also accurate: Our minds can become the place where truths become lies. Our minds are incredibly powerful places. They are made to protect us from bad things, from pain and, sometimes, from truth. This means we have to be very intentional with ourselves about what is true and what is not—both about ourselves and about others. If I can get you to be honest for a moment, what are some of those recurring thoughts that play on a loop through your mind every day?

- Do you feel like you are honest with yourself about the things in your life you do well?
- How about those you do not do well?
- Do you have a sense of how you treat other people you encounter throughout the day?
- Would they agree if someone asked them and they were forced to tell the truth?
- Are you generally kind to yourself?
- Do you treat yourself like you would expect a friend to treat you?

So many of these questions boil down to what we call *self-awareness*. A widely accepted definition of *self-awareness* is the ability to see yourself clearly and objectively through reflection and introspection.[2] While we can never be fully objective about ourselves, self-awareness is a critically important first step on our journey to truth. If we cannot tell the truth to ourselves—the good, the bad, and the ugly—then it's very unlikely we will ever be mature and compassionate enough to tell the truth to others. In the same way, if we cannot receive the truth from ourselves—the good, the bad, and the ugly—then it's very unlikely we will ever be able to receive it from others. As mentioned previously, words matter deeply, which means those words we speak to ourselves, to the tune of 6,200 thoughts a day, matter. They matter a lot. Those truths and lies change us, for better or worse, moment after moment, day after day, and year after year. Courage is learning to tell and accept the truth—first and foremost to ourselves.

Now I want to turn our attention to the truths we do (or do not) tell one another. Somewhere along the way, telling the truth got a reputation for being mean-spirited or in poor taste.

Regardless of how this originated, it seems to have stuck, especially in American culture. This has created an environment in which telling the truth is almost looked down upon. Not only is this absurd and unhealthy, but it is detrimental to our ability to be the best version of ourselves.

Many of us have had an experience where we were humming along thinking everything was just fine when *BAM!* Something came out of nowhere and just flattened us. Little did we know our family and friends around us likely saw it coming, or at least saw signs that it might come, but no one said anything because they were too worried about hurting our feelings. Do you know what is worse than having our feelings hurt? Getting leveled by something we could have avoided if someone had loved us enough to tell us the truth. Do you know what hurts even worse? Never having the chance to be the best version of ourselves because no one around us will tell us the truth about how we can improve and get better. Ouch.

I believe deeply in community and in our need for one another—but never more so than when it comes to having honest feedback from people we trust and who want the very best for us. Having trustworthy, kindhearted, genuine people in our closest circles is an absolute game changer. Transformation cannot happen outside of truthfulness.

> We need to learn to tell one another how things make us feel, to name what we do and do not like, and to plainly ask others to stop doing what hurts us. All these things should be done both respectfully and unapologetically.

We need a new external feedback loop with one another. A feedback loop where kindness and honesty are valued above all. A feedback loop where we sincerely desire to receive and tell the truth to one another because we understand it is the only way to experience growth and progress. We need to learn to tell one another how things make us feel, to name what we do and do not like, and to plainly ask others to stop doing what hurts us. All these things should be done both respectfully and unapologetically. We should not feel the need to stammer in these situations or act as though we are in the wrong for voicing what is true for us. This is called self-advocating, and it is something many parents are trying to teach their children to do from a young age. But it's not just our children who need it—it's a tool that every adult needs to practice regularly too.

My most practical advice for those seeking to tell more truths is to just start doing it. Today. In every conversation. In every relationship. When someone asks you a question, answer them honestly. Not what you think they want to hear, but your truthful answer. When someone asks you how you're doing, answer them honestly. You don't have to go into great detail, but it's perfectly fine to say, "Gosh, I'm feeling tired today. Thank you for asking—that means a lot." What freedom there is in that truthfulness—for all parties involved! Now that person has a chance to come alongside you and check on you and show you compassion. This opportunity would not have existed if you had answered with "I'm fine, thanks."

Now there will be plenty of people in your life who have no interest in this sort of truth telling. They live in a bubble of comfortability that the truth threatens to pop. So do not be surprised when some people stop asking questions simply because they do not want to hear your truthful answers. But also don't be discouraged—tell the truth in kindness and trust that the people who end up around you are the ones who need to be there. The rest are still on the journey, and we want to honor that while not letting it become a roadblock for our own growth.

> Courage is telling the truth.
> One moment at a time.

Hiding our true feelings is the opposite of courage; it is cowardly. It kicks the proverbial can down the road, but it does not solve the problem. In fact, it likely exacerbates the situation in a way that will blow up in our faces at a later time. I am shocked by the freedom we experience when we learn to tell each other the truth in kindness. It is truly the most honoring decision we could make for anyone we care about in life. Courage is telling the truth. One moment at a time. Until we once again become more like little children—who have actually been the ones getting it much closer to right all along. Courage is committing to tell the truth to ourselves, to stop repeating lies about ourselves in our own minds, and to both tell and expect the truth to and from those around us.

My life was forever changed for the better when I started a mentoring relationship with a couple who loved me enough to tell me the truth. The relationship started with them telling me affirming truths about all my gifts. But as our trust in one another grew, they began to feel the relational freedom to tell me other, harder truths too—the sorts of things I did not want to hear but needed to hear. And because I loved and trusted them like crazy, I listened. Now I did not always respond with graciousness at the time. I have been notoriously terrible at receiving constructive feedback from people. But their love for me and investment in me was so undeniable that I simply could not ignore their truths, even if they initially stung. So I listened, I took them to heart, and I grew. I grew into a different and better man—the kind of man who would want to write the book you're holding in your hands. This growth never could have happened without their willingness to tell me the truth. The truth can produce fruit we might never fully understand or be able to measure.

I'd like to end this chapter with a story about a young man who reached out to me recently for advice regarding a very difficult situation. I had two choices: I could play it safe and hold back, which would protect our budding relationship but not his long-term growth, or I could be kind but direct and honest, at the risk that it might hinder or even end our relationship. I chose the latter of the two and kindly told him what I knew was a very hard truth to hear.

He responded to me by saying, "Thank you for being one of the few truth tellers in my life. I feel like I can walk in freedom and honesty with you, with no shame."

My reply: "This is how we were all meant to do life together. We're just not very good at it."

It takes courage for us to tell the truth to ourselves and each other. But the truth *will* set us free. And in that freedom, we will be so much better equipped to use 14 minutes a day to do more good.

NOTES

[1]Jason Murdock, "Humans Have More than 6,000 Thoughts per Day, Psychologists Discover," Newsweek, July 15, 2020, www.newsweek.com /humans-6000-thoughts-every-day-1517963.

[2]Courtney E. Ackerman, "What Is Self-Awareness and Why Is It Important?," Positive Psychology, October 16, 2020, https://positivepsychology .com/self-awareness-matters-how-you-can-be-more-self-aware/.

# CHAPTER FIFTEEN

# "I'm Sorry"

Several years ago, I was invited to speak at a local high school. It was a private Christian school, and I did not get to choose my topic. I was hoping for an easy assignment—something that felt comfortable and fit well in my wheelhouse. Instead, I was given a Bible verse about asking others for forgiveness when we have hurt them. Oh, boy. I do not remember exactly which verse it was or what it said, but I distinctly remember how bothersome it felt to prepare that speech because I was talking about something I was not very good at doing.

How annoying is that? I was being asked to speak to a big group of impressionable high schoolers about a practice that I'd failed miserably at myself. So I did the only thing I knew to do: I showed up, faked my way through the speech, and just pretended that apologies came easily for me.

No, not really. What I really did (with great hesitation and expert stalling techniques every step along the way) was make a short list of a few people I had wronged, people I'd never asked to forgive me, and I reached out to them before I gave the speech.

> Doing the right thing is the right thing, even when people do not respond the way we hope they will.

Sending those emails and making those calls was not easy. I'd like to tell you that everyone I reached out to responded back with grace, kindness, and forgiveness, but that would not be true—and it's okay. Doing the right thing is the right thing, even when people do not respond the way we hope they will. For me, in that moment, I needed to acknowledge that I had hurt someone. What they did with that truth was up to them—it was no longer in my control. But I knew I could not in good conscience stand on a stage and tell high schoolers that we should all have the courage to go to people we have wronged and apologize if I was not first willing to do that myself.

Another one of the most meaningful and important ways we can engage in a billion hours of good is by embracing the humility required to learn to say "I'm sorry" to one another. There are countless ways we can spend our 14 minutes of good a day (as we have been discovering already), but using that time to repair broken relationships is undoubtedly one of the worthiest.

Sometimes we hurt people, usually unintentionally. All of us are guilty of that to some degree. The real question is whether we have the humility, maturity, and courage to seek relational restoration after it happens—that part likely says more about our character than our initial offense. Saying "I'm sorry" is difficult because it requires us to swallow our pride and admit we were wrong. It's also hard because we have no control over how the other person will respond.

In a perfect world, every single person we apologize to would graciously receive our apology with humility and maybe even go as far as to share their own apology for whatever role they might have played in the conflict. But we don't live in a utopia. And more often than we would prefer, the person we apologize to will not be prepared to respond to us as graciously as we approach them. This is not what we would choose, but it is often what we get, which is what makes saying "I'm sorry" so courageous.

In many ways, saying "I'm sorry" is the culmination of several of the other courageous acts we have already discussed. It requires showing up, it is certainly a hard thing we're choosing to do on purpose, and it necessitates our telling the truth—a truth that doesn't make us look very good. In this way, saying "I'm sorry" is the courage trifecta. I can speak for myself in admitting that my penchant for being right is much stronger than my desire to make peace with those I have wronged. But this is what makes those "I'm sorry" moments so powerful—whether we find ourselves on the giving or receiving end of an apology.

I had a friend who was in graduate school at a private university several years ago and recently recounted a story to me that I have not been able to forget. As soon as I decided to include a chapter on saying "I'm sorry" in this book, I knew this was a story I absolutely needed to include. My friend had several part-time jobs during his time in graduate school, and one of them was working as an assistant for one of the associate deans of his school. The nature of his job allowed him to become very close to this associate dean and have a front-row seat for much of this man's life. This scholastic leader was very well regarded in academia—he was kind of a big deal. I say that because it makes the next part of the story even more incredible.

My friend relayed to me that every single evening when this highly accomplished scholar would make his 10-minute drive home, he would drive in silence and walk back through his day from start to finish. During that time, he'd recount each conversation and interaction he'd engaged in throughout the day, whether they were brief hallway introductions or large university board meetings. His entire purpose in going through this exercise every day was to recall if there was anything he had said or done that might have hurt someone. Did he ignore someone in his haste, speak ungraciously, lose his temper, speak unkindly, say too much or too little, gossip, listen to gossip, hold back a kind word or compliment, or any of the other hundreds of ways we all, in our haste, can hurt people?

A couple of parts of this story humble me the most. One is this man's discipline to do this every single day—his ability to make it a true habit and routine of his life says everything you possibly need to know about his character and integrity. But I am also stunned by his humility. I am, in the grand scheme of things, completely unimportant. Yet I find myself "big timing" people too often—a phrase I use to describe what happens when we believe our success or importance gives us a pass on giving someone else our full attention, time, or energy. Now I'm not saying that this man did not have to turn down meetings or defer people to his colleagues or assistants. I am not suggesting that he said "yes" to every single request made of him. Not at all. I am suggesting that he clearly resolved to practice true kindness and humility in every interaction he had each day—to the extent that he would hold himself accountable for the times when he had not shown those qualities so that he could reach out to that person and say "I'm sorry." That is the kind of person I want to work for, work with, be led by, and actually become myself. That is courage in action, and it is both stunning and inspiring to hear about it in real life.

I want to let you in on a little secret—saying "I'm sorry" is definitely courageous, but it's also mutually beneficial. Because the weight of broken relationships and strained bonds get piled into an enormous bag we carry everywhere we go, which will eventually crush us under its weight if we allow it to do so. Having the courage to go to those whom we have hurt and say "I'm sorry" gives us the opportunity to take one pound of weight at a time out of that bag until we can eventually drop the bag altogether. Then we can live in true peace—with ourselves and those around us. I want to reiterate again that leaving this weight behind has nothing to do with how our apologies are received. Those hurt feelings and apologies are left behind the moment we make peace, regardless of whether our olive branch is received or broken in two over the person's knee like a Bo Jackson baseball bat.

> I want to let you in on a little secret—
> saying "I'm sorry" is definitely courageous,
> but it's also mutually beneficial.

I recently read a story about a man who sought out a former teacher and apologized to him 39 years after treating him poorly during a class in junior high. Thirty-nine years! This particular story had a lovely ending because the retired teacher and former student began a new friendship as adults; but even if it had not led to that reconciliation, the student in the story needed to say "I'm sorry" because he had been carrying an unnecessary burden and weight around for almost 40 years. Ironically, the man was inspired to find and apologize to his former teacher when the man's brother-in-law admitted to him several years after his wedding that he had not really liked him originally and tried to talk his sister out of marrying him because of his ethnicity. What courage for the brother-in-law to admit that! And what does courage do? It begets more courage, which led to the unlikely stories I recounted here. What a gift.

For those of us who are parents, one of the greatest gifts we can give our children is to model for them what it looks like to say, "I'm sorry. I messed up. Please forgive me." Especially if we are willing to say these words (and mean them) to our kids themselves. These eight simple words hold the power and possibility of showing our kids what humility, grace, and courage look like in real life. If we want our children to become teenagers and adults who can give and receive grace, we have to model for them what this kind of courage looks like.

> If we want our children to become teenagers and adults who can give and receive grace, we have to model for them what this kind of courage looks like.

I have four young kids (ages 2, 5, 8, and 10 at the writing of this book), and I can assure you that at those ages and with my inclination for impatience, I have good reason to apologize to them every single day. For better or worse (often worse), I have very high expectations for my children's behavior, which can certainly be a good thing but can also be a curse when my exacting demands are developmentally inappropriate. Thankfully, my dear friend Jeremy Dew, who is a therapist primarily working with children and families, introduced me to the idea of repairing relationships with our children. This is fancy therapist talk for sucking it up and saying "I'm sorry" to our children when we mess up. It is something that my wife and I try to do when we are unkind, impatient, don't listen, or any of the other mistakes we make as we parent.

We hope our children are learning from us that it's better than okay to say "I'm sorry." We hope they are learning that apologies are part of being an emotionally mature, self-reflective, and kind human being. We hope they are learning that expressing sincere remorse is part of our choosing to live with courage, both in our home and outside of it, with those we've hurt just a little and those we've hurt a lot, and with people who accept our apologies and those who choose not to.

> Saying "I'm sorry" is a true act of courage and
> good—one that requires us to be reflective about
> those we may have hurt, authentic in our apology,
> and willing to be okay if our words are not received
> in a way that matches our desire to make peace.

Saying "I'm sorry" is a true act of courage and good—one that requires us to be reflective about those we may have hurt, authentic in our apology, and willing to be okay if our words are not received in a way that matches our desire to make peace. It is a necessary step in our moving forward, unencumbered by the extra weight.

Now that we have found our courage, shown up, done hard things (on purpose), failed and gotten back up, told the truth, and said "I'm sorry," it is time for the next step in our journey to a billion hours of good: uncovering the creative problem solving that has been inside us all along.

This is where our compassion and courage put on their work gloves and go out into the world to do more good. We've laid the groundwork, and now we get to see the fruit of that internal work create a lasting impact on the lives of others.

## Reflections on Courage
1. Do you have a North Star?
2. Do your calendar and credit card statements support this being your true North Star?
3. Do you find it difficult to show up in new places to try new things?
4. If so, why do you think that is?
5. How did you feel when reading the chapter about doing hard things?

6. What are some of the difficult or uncomfortable things you tend to avoid?
7. What is it about failing that scares you the most?
8. What is one specific way the fear of failing is holding you back in life right now?
9. Why do you think we find the truth to be such a slippery watermelon?
10. Do you struggle more with telling the truth to others or hearing it about yourself?
11. Do you find it difficult to admit when you're wrong? Why or why not?
12. How did you feel when you read the story about the man who mentally walked back through each day to make sure he hadn't unintentionally hurt anyone?

PART II

# CREATIVITY
# AND CHANGE

# CHAPTER SIXTEEN

# Creativity Is
# for Everyone

We receive the gifts of courage and compassion with open hands for one reason—so we can then give them back to the world with those same open hands. We do this with hopes that each of us can leave things better than we found them. I know this may seem lofty to you, but that is exactly the goal of a billion hours of good: to empower every single one of us to take our newfound compassion and courage into the world in such a way that it does good, 14 minutes at a time.

> We receive the gifts of courage and compassion with
> open hands for one reason—so we can then give
> them back to the world with those same open hands.

The key to this step of the process is creativity.

First, we must acknowledge a few things about creativity that may have caused many of us some degree of difficulty over the years. Namely, most of us do not actually believe we are all that creative. Maybe someone told us this at one point, or maybe we just told ourselves this at some point, but somewhere along the way, many of us have come to believe that creativity is not a trait we possess.

Similar to a child who once loved baseball but eventually had to come to terms with the reality that he or she was not going to be a professional baseball player, we seem to treat creativity in this same way. "I'm just not creative," we declare, and then we move on to other things. The truth is that each one of us has some level of creativity. In fact, you will learn soon that one study shows 98 percent of five-year-old children tested at a "creative genius" level! We will talk more about what children can teach us about creativity, but before we do that, I want to first name and then dispel the myth that you "just aren't creative." A convenient excuse sometimes? Certainly. But not a statement based in truth.

For many of us, the basis of the idea that we are "just not creative" stems from the misconception that "creative" is synonymous with "art." Therefore, when someone mentions the word "creativity," we may be reminded of that clay vase we gave to our grandmother one Christmas that was so oddly shaped she actually mistook it for an ashtray (despite the fact that she didn't smoke). Or perhaps it taps into an unpleasant experience with art in our adult years. My four young children get a real kick out of watching me draw because Dad, who is extremely competitive and strongly prefers success at anything he tries, suddenly sticks his tongue out like Michael Jordan, focuses with the intensity I imagine Picasso or Rembrandt might have shown, and still ends up drawing something that resembles abstract art but not at all on purpose. Sign me up for any challenge in which I may have to spell words backward, do mental math in my head, hum a tune, or even act something out, but you'll get a hearty sigh from me when drawing is involved.

If you feel the same way as I do about all-things art, then you might also get a lump in your throat when someone mentions the word *creativity*.

The good news for you (and me) is that creativity is so much bigger than art. It certainly comes out in beautiful paintings, sculptures, and graphic designs, but it comes out in a million other ways too. Creativity is on display every single day in buildings and backyards, in churches and charities, in newsrooms and class-rooms, and in recording booths and restaurants. Anywhere you find people, you might also find creativity. Now, this isn't to say that everywhere you find people you will find creativity. That is certainly not true. But we're certainly all qualified to create.

There are several definitions of creativity, some more help-ful than others. But the one I like most is from the Cambridge Dictionary, which reads, "Creativity is the ability to produce or use original and unusual ideas." Notice no mention of paintbrushes or pottery wheels. Another definition of creativity starts with, "The use of the imagination . . ." I really love this one.[1]

Creativity, at its core, is the use of our imaginations to produce something new. That's it. Each one of us is qualified to do that. So here's our challenge—when we do allow ourselves to create a new idea, we cannot let those creative thoughts stay locked in our own brains forever or they won't be able to do much good. The ideas birthed in our imaginations must, at some point, take root in the world around us in a real way.

> Creativity, at its core, is the use of our imaginations to produce something new.

Creativity walks hand in hand with its closest friend, curiosity.

Creativity pairs up with its biological sister, innovation, to find new solutions.

Creativity jumps out of bed every morning to answer the question, "Why not?"

Creativity is a conscious choice to see the world not as it is but as it could be.

Compassion and courage give birth to creativity when we decide (1) we care enough about the pain points in the world around us to imagine and then act on a better way forward, and (2) we will no longer be frozen by our fear of failing.

Creativity does not discriminate based on age, gender, education, socioeconomic status, race, sexual orientation, or religion. It is for everyone. Inside of everyone. And everyone includes *you*. So let's unlock your internal creativity into a billion hours of good.

### NOTE

[1]Lexico, s.v., "creativity," www.lexico.com/en/definition/creativity.

# CHAPTER SEVENTEEN

# Creativity as Currency

Before we talk about how best to activate this creativity that lives inside of us, I want to spend just a few minutes talking about why creativity matters and what makes it so valuable. It does not seem difficult to understand why all of us would do well to grow in both our courage and our compassion. But creativity? Is it really that important? My resounding answer is "Yes, yes, yes, one hundred times yes." Let me show you why.

> If courage is finding our North Star, and compassion is mapping out our route, creativity is where we actually start to drive to where we want to go.

If courage is finding our North Star, and compassion is mapping out our route, creativity is where we actually start to drive to where we want to go. Creativity is the ability to look at a problem in a new and fresh way. It takes compassion for us to care about the problem, it takes courage for us to show up to see and engage the problem, but it takes creativity to actually solve the problem. Without creativity, our dreams never leave the dream stage—they stay in our minds forever as ideas, hopes, and possibilities that never fully turn into solutions.

At a time when we can buy practically anything and even have it delivered to our doorsteps in two days or less, creativity is more valuable than ever because it cannot be bought. If we could buy it, the value would be both cheapened and diluted, which is exactly why the opposite has happened. As more and more products and services have become commoditized, the value of those things that cannot be packaged and delivered instantaneously has skyrocketed. Creativity is the most valuable currency we could possibly possess. More than bitcoin, stocks, cash, or even the stability of our current job.

Having a rainy-day fund or plush bank account is great, but creativity gives us the ability to refill that rainy-day fund over and over for the rest of our lives.

Having a stable job is great, but even the most secure career could be gone at any second. The long-term value we hold is in our ability to creatively come up with new ways of making money to support our families, and that's a skill that can never be taken away from us.

Having the solution to a single difficult problem is great, but we are typically asked to solve hundreds of problems every day. Creativity gives us the ability to solve problems both large and small.

Creativity is a currency that never runs out, never falls out of season, and never loses its value. It's what separates dreamers from doers, driving innovation, as far back as we have a historical record. From hieroglyphics on stone walls to the present-day tech innovations, creativity has solved more problems, saved more lives, and made life better for billions of people. It is truly invaluable, and it is a tool every single one of us already possesses.

> Creativity is a currency that never runs out, never falls out of season, and never loses its value.

But are we leveraging our creativity as fully and powerfully as possible? Probably not.

In many cases, we fail to make the most of our creativity because we do not fully appreciate how valuable it can be, or we have not learned how to harness its power.

One of the most beautiful parts of the recent COVID-19 pandemic was seeing all the creativity burst forth. In just a matter of days, we had massive manufacturing facilities pivoting to make personal protective equipment for health care workers, legions of people stuck at home cranking out homemade facemasks, and factories suddenly producing thousands of gallons of hand sanitizer. Artists took to the internet to put on impromptu living room concerts, teachers learned how to use online educational tools, and restaurants quickly discovered ways to feed thousands of people while allowing them to remain in the safety of their homes or vehicles. If we were paying attention at all, it was impossible to miss all the little sparks of creativity floating around at a time when the world seemed to be engulfed in darkness. These courageous people who dared to tap into their creativity and offer solutions to the world were, in many ways, shining as sources of light during a time when others were frozen by fear and anxiety.

I was personally fortunate enough to be involved in two projects during the COVID-19 pandemic that required just the slightest spark of creativity to get off the ground. The first was an idea I had when I initially discovered that my children were going to be out of school for what we thought at the time would be a few weeks. My children were 2, 5, 8, and 10 years old, and I knew keeping them educated and entertained without leaving the house was going to be a tall order for my wife Stacey especially, as I continued with a mostly normal work schedule. So I reached out to a few friends and asked if they might go live with me on Facebook to host a fun and educational virtual field trip for kids and parents stuck at home during the pandemic.

My generous friends said, "Sure," and the rest is history.

I posted a simple message on my personal Facebook page asking if any of my friends who were parents might be interested in tuning in for something like this with their kids, so that I could begin to figure out exactly how to stream what I called Afternoon Adventures. I hit send on the post on a Saturday morning, and by Monday at noon, more than 25,000 families had RSVP'd that they would like to tune in and watch.

When we went live for the first time that afternoon with my exotic-animal veterinarian friend Dr. Brittni Turner, 12,000 people were tuned in to the live stream as she awed us with the beauty of a large family of giraffes. Within just a few days, that video was viewed more than 500,000 times by people all across the world. It also brought more than 30,000 new families to my public author/ speaker Facebook page (where I ended up streaming the videos). This was an incredible, yet unintended, consequence of the initial creative idea.

We ended up airing six straight weeks of Afternoon Adventures (30 total), which included visits with giraffes, field trips to police stations, explorations in art, experiments with cooking, lessons about sign language, tours of fire stations, and a behind-the-scenes look at pizza parlors. All told, the six weeks of videos racked up more than one million views. Talk about a big table with a bunch of new chairs pulled up!

I want to point out here that my creativity cost absolutely nothing. In fact, it became profitable as I found weekly sponsors. My creativity caused no harm, and it helped solve a problem that every single family in America (and many across the world) were facing during quarantine. I was not unique in seeing the problem, but I leveraged creativity to offer a real, practical solution to a problem many others were facing.

There is no reason every school district in America could not have done what I did. You could even make the argument they were better equipped to do so, with full teams of multimedia professionals and a host of talented teachers looking for ways to virtually help. But I was the one who quickly brought the solution to the market, and the market responded positively. Sometimes creative ideas turn out beautifully, as was the case with Afternoon Adventures. Sometimes they fail beautifully. But every idea that is never tried fails.

> Sometimes creative ideas turn out beautifully, as was the case with Afternoon Adventures. Sometimes they fail beautifully. But every idea that is never tried fails.

The second project I was able to be a part of during quarantine was to help launch a community-wide relief fund to help small businesses in our town survive the shutdown. I was feeling really burdened by the plight of so many of my neighbors and friends, just like many of you probably were too, but I didn't know what I could do to help. Then, one morning, my friend Chris reached out and asked if I wanted to help him come up with T-shirt designs or something we could try to sell to raise money. While I didn't think T-shirts were the answer, Chris's idea was just the kick in the butt I needed. We all felt like we wanted to do something to help our community members in danger of losing their livelihoods, and we needed a strong and collective effort to inspire others to get involved.

That same morning, I called the CEO of our local United Way (a woman named Alison, whom I'd never spoken to before). I also reached out to the CEO of our Community Foundation, Patricia.

I pitched to both of them an idea for the three of us to put our collective heads and hearts together to help our community in a unified way. By the end of the day, they both said, "Yes, we're in."

Within 72 hours, the three of us launched a community relief fund in partnership with every major local media outlet, our city officials, and our local Chamber of Commerce. In just about 8 weeks, our relief fund raised and distributed about $1.2 million to local businesses, to keep their employees from being laid off, and to local nonprofits who were directly meeting the needs of those who had already lost their jobs in the wake of the pandemic.

Again, every single person I knew was hoping and wishing we could do something to help those we knew were struggling. What we did was offer a tangible and united solution. Our creativity was in our partnership and in our moving quickly so that we could help stop the bleeding before it was too late.

I knew that I could personally start a fundraiser that would probably have a little bit of success. Maybe I could raise tens of thousands of dollars—a hundred thousand at the absolute most. That money would certainly be helpful to whoever received it, but it wouldn't be as far-reaching and widespread as it could be if I partnered with the right people. So I called two of the biggest names in my community and asked them to partner with me. I knew Alison with United Way and Patricia with the Community Foundation both had the reputation of being movers and shakers. They knew the right people, they had the right people on their boards, and most importantly, they knew how to get help to the right people. I also knew we all shared the same heart for wanting to offer immediate and sustainable help to people in our community. Together, we used our courage, compassion, and creativity to bring good to the world through a united partnership that raised and distributed money quickly, efficiently, and with appropriate oversight.

Raising money to help others is not necessarily creative in and of itself. But doing it with an emphasis on partnership (the two organizations I called had not partnered on a project in years) and with an appropriate level of urgency and accuracy were the keys to the project's success. By our last count, the small business and nonprofit grants we administered had directly impacted more than 34,000 people in our community and saved nearly 600 jobs.

It all started with an idea. Then a phone call. Then a second call. Actually, it started when my friend Chris cared enough to message me about us doing something to help. His message to me was the first domino to fall, and that resulted in many, many deserving people being helped.

Again, I am using real examples from my personal life as a way to encourage you that the power of creativity is real and tangible. It truly has the capacity to change the world—not as ideas stuck inside of us but as a form of actions that go out from us. The stories I mentioned here required no advanced degree or thousands of dollars. They only needed an ounce of creativity, the courage to show up, and the compassion to want to make a difference. Every one of us possesses each of those.

I am sincere when I say every single person reading this book could have been the catalyst behind those two stories. It certainly benefitted me to have a good reputation and credibility in my community, and when I launched Afternoon Adventures, it didn't hurt that I had an above-average sized social media reach, but how do you think those things came to be? It wasn't by accident or pure luck. They were built over thousands of small acts of courage, compassion, and creativity with no fanfare and no intention by me other than to do as much good as I could when I could.

These were not my first creative ideas, and they almost certainly will not be my last. Each successful idea and the execution of that idea earned me credibility and trust, which will make my next idea easier because people have seen my previous successes and will be more willing to jump in sooner the next time.

This is why creativity is such a valuable currency. It draws people to our ideas because they believe the ideas will help solve real problems. To prove this point about building up this kind of trust from people, I engaged in a small experiment while working on this chapter. One afternoon, I jumped onto my personal Facebook page and made the following post verbatim (I made it public if you want to search my name and look at the May 25, 2020, post):

An experiment for the book I'm writing right now:

If I told you I had a new idea, and it was truly going to change the world for the better, and it would cost you no money and only a little bit of time to be a part of it with me, would you commit to helping without knowing anything else? Simply like this post if you would choose to help. I am looking for one hundred people to join me.

PS: No geographical or age restrictions.

Then I logged off and went back to writing more of this chapter. By the time I checked back a little more than half an hour later, nearly 50 people liked the post and/or commented to say, "I'm in." By the end of the day, it was close to one hundred.

In for what? They didn't know. But they trusted me, and they trusted the power of creativity as a force for good in the world. How many more would jump in and sign up once the actual idea was revealed? Many. How many more would jump in if personally contacted by email, phone, or text? Many. How much does that number grow with each successful idea and execution? By a lot.

This is why I believe creativity is greatly undervalued as a currency for changing the world.

This creativity lives inside each of us, is an incredibly powerful tool and currency, and is the conduit of turning our courage and compassion into meaningful change. In fact, I believe it is the secret sauce to turning our 14 minutes of good a day into a tidal wave of positive transformation. So why does it sometimes feel so hard to be creative?

# Cardboard Boxes

If you've ever been with children for any length of time, then you know full well that creativity is alive and well in childhood. When children are involved, anything and everything can become something else at the drop of a hat. Even the same thing can morph into 5, 10, or 20 different things in just a matter of minutes. The best part is when you ask a child, "Wait, I thought that was a [fill in the blank]." The child looks at you and says, in an exasperated tone, "That's what it *used* to be. But now it's a [fill in the blank] because all the lions came and took it back to their colony to watch cartoons." I bet more than a few of you are nodding along at that example because you know it is absolutely true.

In the 1960s, George Land and Beth Jarman were hired to develop a creativity test to help NASA identify the most innovative engineers and scientists. Land and Jarman did that quite well, and a few years later, in 1968, they decided to take a basic form of that same test and give it to children. They started with a group of

1,600 children, ages 4 and 5. The purpose of the test was to have the children look at an age-appropriate problem and come up with new, different, and innovative ideas for solving it. This is creativity in a nutshell. An astounding 98 percent of those 4- and 5-year-old children tested at the "genius level" of creativity. The results were so stunning that Land and Jarman decided to extend the study and test the same group of children again at ages 10 and 15. At 10 years old, just 30 percent of the children now tested at the genius level of creativity. By age 15, that number was just 12 percent. When they gave that same test to nearly 300,000 adults, a mere 2 percent tested at the genius level of creativity.[1]

In some ways, these numbers can feel disheartening because the data seem to strongly suggest the vast majority of us have lost that innate ability to be creative. But I don't view it in that way at all. I am encouraged to consider that we are seeking to rediscover something that almost every single 4- and 5-year-old already has. I am encouraged to know that to become more creative, we have to become more like 4- and 5-year-old children. Any of us can do that—especially for just 14 minutes a day!

To understand the innate creativity of children, we only have to look as far as a cardboard box. Parents often joke that kids get more enjoyment out of a simple cardboard box than they do the expensive toy that came in the box. But, honestly, this isn't a joke at all. Children love cardboard boxes because they are limitless, whereas a toy is usually limited to serving just one purpose or representing just one thing. In other words, most toys actually limit the creativity of a child because they come with a very clear and specific use that includes certain boundaries. Because the nature of a toy is something specific, it is no longer able to become all the other creations that can form in a child's imagination.

I am guilty of this as a parent when I say things to my children like, "Why are you using that toy in that way? That's not what it's for." But a cardboard box is just the opposite. Free of those "rules" and "conditions," children are able to let their imaginations run wild! The next thing you know, they're turning that cardboard box into a rocket, a cave, a slide, a shield, a sword, a car, a ship, and a hundred other things until the box eventually becomes so torn up that it is carried out of the house in pieces. So what do children and cardboard boxes have to do with our creativity? Everything.

Scientists tell us there are two types of thinking processes when it comes to creativity.[2] The first is called *convergent thinking*, which is almost exclusively what we learn in formal education. (Some even make the case that our methods of teaching and learning in school are why children lose their creative genius as they grow older.) Convergent thinking is essentially a gathering of all the facts and data to attain the single most "correct" answer.

*Divergent thinking*, on the other hand, often happens on the fringes of our minds, or even in our subconscious, and is used to produce creative ideas by exploring as many possible solutions as possible. Divergent thinking is more about the journey than the destination; it is where the process is often valued over correctness.

> Very early on, we are trained to find the "correct" answer, which teaches us there is only one way of thinking about things.

As adults, the vast majority of us use convergent thinking as our primary means of solving a problem. It is our default. We gather the facts and data in front of us and make a decision based on what is most "correct." We learn to do this in school when the majority of our tests are multiple-choice. When the answer choices are A, B, C, or D, they do not leave much room for divergent thinking. We are certainly not rewarded for circling both B and C and writing a paragraph below explaining how the answer is usually somewhere in the middle because of the inherent complexity of understanding human emotions and intrinsic motivation. Our teachers might have smirked when they saw an answer like that, and they almost certainly would have followed the smirk up with a bright red X. So very early on, we are trained to find the "correct" answer, which teaches us there is only one way of thinking about things.

This inadvertently stifles the part of our minds that comes up with innovative and creative solutions because we are no longer using that muscle. When we stop using that muscle, it becomes weaker; as it becomes weaker, it becomes harder to muster; and as it becomes harder to muster, we use it less.

You can see the vicious cycle. But it does not have to be this way. Just as a muscle can atrophy from lack of use, it can also grow from intentional use—such is the case with creativity, our minds, and our use of divergent thinking.

> Just as a muscle can atrophy from lack of use, it can also grow from intentional use—such is the case with creativity, our minds, and our use of divergent thinking.

My friend Corey, who used to work for Nike in Beaverton, Oregon, once told me that most of his creative ideas start out as silliness. He went on to say that at his very best, when he gives these seemingly silly ideas space to grow and be nurtured, they often turn into his very best ideas. His challenge is shared by most of us: he doesn't have enough space to come up with his silly ideas in the first place, and he doesn't give the silly ideas he does manage to come up with enough space to grow into something sustainable and workable. I'll come back to those points in a moment, but I first want to note that I love his use of the word "silly" here because I believe it reminds us of something important.

As adults, we often view the word "silly" negatively. Our perception of something being silly suggests it is impractical or childish. But that's exactly the goal of this exercise for us! Childish and silly ideas are usually much closer to divergent thinking and therefore serve as the starting place for true creativity. When a child says something is silly, they say it in a way that is full of laughter and playfulness. Being silly, or thinking silly, is a part of play. When we play, we think divergently. Silly is good. Silly means we're not taking ourselves so seriously, which gives us a chance to actually begin the creative process that has become so foreign for many of us.

My friend Corey comes up with creative ideas not by accident but because he dares to be silly! This is what happens when we allow ourselves to play, run around, and free our minds from the imprisonment of what has already been created. It's only in silliness and play that we can begin to generate new ideas that are truly creative. But being silly is a choice, and it will require a level of intentionality and thoughtfulness that many of us fail to execute because busyness is our default setting. We must remember that silliness is where the magic happens. And that magic will only happen when we make space for it.

When I say we should make more time for play and silliness, I don't mean signing up for an adult flag football league or adding on a weekend gig as a clown. Those things might sound really fun to you, and if so, I would encourage you to engage in them. But play is so much bigger than that. Playfulness, in the way I am describing it, means intentionally and consistently getting out of our comfort zones to do new things.

Play can be going on a slow walk or a fast run, planting a garden or mowing the lawn, shooting baskets at the park or learning to weave a basket, building a pillow fort or constructing a birdhouse. Play happens when we stop taking ourselves seriously and allow ourselves to let loose.

> When we break from our typical routines
> and habits, we discover that our minds will
> also break free from the routines and
> habits it has created as well.

When we break from our typical routines and habits, we discover that our minds will also break free from the routines and habits it has created as well. Anything we do that engages our senses in new ways is likely to lead us to new experiences and thoughts, and thus is more likely to help us experience creativity. Newness begets newness, and that is the heart of creativity—using our imaginations to create or produce new things. This is incredibly difficult to do when we are rarely putting ourselves in a position to experience and feel new things.

There is a reason many of our most brilliant ideas come to us while we're in the shower, driving home, taking a run, or even sleeping! What do each of these moments have in common? They are all moments in which our brains are free from convergent thinking and thereby find the opportunity to use that fringe, subconscious part of our minds that more creative, divergent thinking requires. This is the power of play. This is the beauty of making space for silliness when it comes to engaging the process of creativity.

But how do we brainstorm and come up with creative ideas in a group or organizational setting? How do church leadership teams, school administrators, nonprofit boards, and business management teams translate playing and silliness into a productive project? Are we supposed to go for a group run, skydive as a team, build a pillow fort together in the breakroom? Honestly, those aren't terrible ideas, and I think most every organization would find it beneficial to team culture to make time for just being together without a work-specific goal to accomplish. But that's more about team building than creativity. And those once-a-quarter (at best) team-building exercises will never replace the number of times we'll gather with other adults (informally or formally), coworkers, or community members to try and solve a difficult problem.

So how do we create a team environment in which we are more likely to "use our imaginations to create or produce new things"? What can we learn from children and cardboard boxes and silliness and play that will translate into real-world solutions for the problems that affect other people the most? How can we foster this kind of limitless creativity within our corporate offices, churches, and nonprofits so we propel our systems forward with the most innovative and original ideas available today?

Let me start with the short answer and then expound from there. To birth creativity in our organizations, we must strive to create environments in which no one feels inferior or foolish about bringing an idea to the table. This almost always starts with the leadership, and I can assure you I have not always done this well.

> To birth creativity in our organizations, we must strive to create environments in which no one feels inferior or foolish about bringing an idea to the table.

One of the most painful pieces of feedback I ever received was secondhand but corroborated through a strange triangle of mutual relationships. The crux of the feedback was that my brashness and confidence had made two different employees, in two completely different ventures, both feel like I believed I could do their jobs better than they could. Ouch! That is the opposite of how we want people to feel in the environments we foster. And while most negative pieces of feedback can be hard to hear, this one was especially so because the employees hadn't even felt comfortable enough to say this to me directly. This was an all-around leadership failure for me, and I knew it.

When people feel unappreciated, disrespected, unheard, and generally overlooked, there is virtually no chance they will take the risk of being creative. Who wants to make space for "silly" when the other people at the table are self-proclaimed experts at deciding which jokes are funny and which ones are not? This is not about humoring one another; it's about honoring one another. It is a culture we must work to create and maintain at all costs.

If you're not in a leadership position and your bosses do not create space for the team to gather together and be creative, this is worth a conversation. The good news is that if the rest of the team will be engaging and generous in their feedback with one another during these kinds of creative discussions, then leadership will often follow suit. Sometimes it might take the gentle nudge of, "Hey Bob, I know we've got a few other things to cover, but I really think 5–10 more minutes of this important conversation could be very valuable to our team."

The vast majority of leaders are going to hear the message beneath that message, which is "Slow down, buddy. Something good is happening here, and you're about to plow right through it."

The other critical way we bring this creativity into our organizations is by just doing it. I know that sounds like a variant of "Suck it up and get it done," but that's really not the point I'm making here. My friend Dr. Eddie Coulson travels around the state of Texas working with thousands of principals and assistant principals at some of the largest school districts in the state. I love how he describes the idea of organizational creativity: "The first idea is almost never the best idea, but it is usually the most important idea, because it gets the conversation started." Read that through one more time before we go on. Dr. Coulson's wisdom here is profound, and he says it in a way that we can easily remember. Let me say it back to you another way that might be helpful: We can't get to the best idea or solution if we don't start with whatever idea or solution we have right now. This is at the heart of a billion hours of good that we've been discussing since the start of this book. It all starts where we are and with what we have. It's the same with creativity and creative ideas.

> "The first idea is almost never the best idea, but it is usually the most important idea, because it gets the conversation started."

Sometimes we are so concerned about our ideas being perfect that we never actually share them. We ponder and process but never share. In those group settings, with a team of people who honor and care about one another and have a shared desire to solve real problems together, someone having the courage to throw out the first idea is often all that is needed to spark the discussion that leads to the final solution.

Almost nothing we see in its final form is anything like the first iteration of that idea or product. You would not recognize the rough draft of this book as being the same project that you're holding in your hands now. But there would be nothing for you to hold in your hands if I had allowed the fear of not writing a perfect rough draft keep me from writing at all. The first idea is almost never the best idea, but it is usually the most important idea because it gets the conversation started.

On the very day I finished the rough draft of this chapter, I walked upstairs to put our five-year-old son to bed and found a new book sitting on his nightstand. I had never seen this book before, but it's called *Not a Box* and was written by Antoinette Portis. The endearing story is about a bunny-like creature who keeps being asked by someone, presumably an adult like us whose creative genius has been stifled, why he keeps doing things with a cardboard box. Why is he sitting in it, standing on it, spraying it with water, wearing it, and so forth? Each time, the bunny responds more adamantly with "It's not a box!" as the accompanying illustration shows him driving a race car, flying a rocket, putting out a big fire, and so on.

This overwhelmingly simple but powerful story not only validates what I wrote earlier about children and boxes; it also reminds us again that the power of creativity is in believing we are capable of making something out of nothing. Once we believe whatever we're working on is "not just a box," there is truly no limit to what we're able to accomplish. It's not a box; it's a rocket. It's not a problem; it's a growth opportunity. It's not a box; it's a race car. It's not an angry customer; it's a chance for honest feedback from someone who uses our product. It's not a box; it's a tall building on fire. It's not a fight with our spouse; it's a possibility for deeper connection and better communication. Maybe the phrase "It's not a box" should make its way into more of our leadership conversations and organizational meetings as we remind one another that what we see does not have to be what we get when it comes to creativity.

So we've created space to play and use our imaginations. We've gathered together to transform our first idea into our best idea. We've even gone as far as to understand that the statement "It's not a box" might give us a powerful new paradigm for seeing the world. Now how do we take that big, scary, hard to wrap our minds-around idea and turn it into a plan that we can understand, believe in, and convince others to join in on so that we can begin to usher in real change, 14 minutes at a time?

## Reflections on Creativity
1. Before reading this section, how did you feel when you heard the word *creativity*?
2. Has that changed at all? Why or why not?

3. Do you believe creativity is really accessible for all of us?
4. Have you ever thought of creativity as currency?
5. What were some of the most creative acts you witnessed during the COVID-19 crisis?
6. How did you react when you read the story of the NASA creativity researchers?
7. Have you ever had a "cardboard box creativity" moment with a child in your life?
8. Do you regularly engage in play and silliness? If not, why?
9. Do play and creativity come easily for your team or organization? If not, what is the bottleneck that keeps that from happening more regularly?
10. How might the phrase "It's not a box" work its way into your life in a way that would be helpful?

### NOTES

[1]Larry Vint, "Fresh Thinking Drives Creativity & Innovation," *QUICK: Journal of the Queensland Society for Information Technology in Education*, 2005, https://research-repository.griffith.edu.au/bitstream/handle/10072/7880/33187_1.pdf.

[2]Praveen Shrestha, "Convergent vs Divergent Thinking," Psychestudy, November 17, 2017, www.psychestudy.com/cognitive/thinking/convergent-vs-divergent.

# CHAPTER NINETEEN

# From Ideation
# to Execution

During the writing of this book, I polled a few dozen friends on their biggest challenges when it came to turning creativity into real change. My exact question was: "When it comes to creativity, what do you need to solve that problem you've always wanted to solve?"

Among their answers were two consistent themes summed up in the following quotes:

- "It would be helpful to learn about keeping dreams big but with manageable steps."
- "I want to know how to share my creative visions with others and get them on board instead of immediately dismissing [my big ideas] as too far-fetched."

These are the exact questions the next two chapters are going to answer. My intention is to make these two chapters the "meat and potatoes" of the entire book. If you've skipped everything else, you should be able to turn to these chapters and immediately be more equipped to take a big, creative idea and start turning it into reality, 14 minutes at a time. Think of these chapters as your step-by-step guide to turning real challenges into new opportunities—for taking an accepted norm and transforming it into a previously unimagined future.

Let's start with the first one: How do we take a big, creative idea and turn it into manageable steps?

I'll begin with a personal story. I remember how overwhelmed I felt when we decided to start Mercy Project, our anti-child-trafficking nonprofit in Ghana, Africa. I had a million questions and no idea where to start. So I did what any reasonable person would do: I got on the internet, opened up my favorite browser, and began my search for information. From there, I spent weeks and weeks learning everything I could about human trafficking, child trafficking, trafficking in Ghana, and Lake Volta (where many trafficked children work in Ghana). I found obscure government documents, traveler blogs, small nonprofits, huge nonprofits, enormous government programs, news stories, and more. I read and read, and slowly, after weeks passed, a picture began to formulate in my mind about what was happening in Ghana. I took all these independent pieces, some more valuable than others, and turned them into a puzzle that gave me a snapshot of deeper understanding.

Let me be clear: Relative to what I know today after 10 years, 40 plus trips to Ghana, and with a staff of 15 Ghanaians, I knew nothing. But I knew more than when I'd started. Most importantly, I knew enough that I was now the expert on this specific, niche topic in 99 percent of the conversations I would find myself in. Please don't miss this. I did not know everything, and I still do not and never will, but I knew enough to accurately and respectfully tell the story, and I knew enough to help others feel confident in my leadership on the topic.

My big, creative idea was that I wanted to help children in Ghana who had been trafficked into the fishing industry on Lake Volta.

My big, creative idea was that I wanted to help children in Ghana who had been trafficked into the fishing industry on Lake Volta.

My very first step was to become as much of an expert as I could on why the problem existed in the first place. This step is not enticing or flashy, and it is unlikely to impress very many people. In fact, you're more likely to bore your friends and family than excite them as you take a dive deep into whatever it is that you're feeling impassioned about. This is par for the course—press on. Most of us are shallow people who know just a little about many different things. "An inch deep and a mile wide," as Edgar Nye first said. This must change if you're committed to seeing a big idea come to life. You must go deeper. And when you think you've gone deep enough, dig down another few feet. This is your starting place.

When we do this kind of deep dive on a creative idea, it serves countless purposes. We would be foolish and cause ourselves unnecessary pain to try and solve a problem or bring a big idea to life without taking this first step. It would be like going skydiving and hoping the parachute attached to us was packed correctly. It certainly could turn out to be, but it feels worth the 10 extra minutes to check (and double-check!) before getting on that plane. In the grand scheme of things, a few weeks of deep diving into something we're interested in doing is truly the equivalent of taking 10 minutes to check our parachutes.

As I mentioned before, enormous credibility comes with being able to effectively "tell the story" of your problem/solution/big idea. In the next chapter, we're going to talk about getting people behind your big idea. Making yourself an expert is the absolute first step in that process. When people ask simple questions like "When did this situation start?" or "Why is this situation happening?" or "Who else has done something like this?" we had better be prepared to offer good, solid, confident answers if we want these people to trust in us and support our solutions.

Additionally, doing this deep dive gives us an opportunity to walk 360 degrees around a problem. Each one of us approaches problems with our own biases and perceptions. This deep dive helps us begin to peel back those layers and offers us an objectivity we simply cannot gain without extensive knowledge.

Becoming educated on a problem helps remove the associated emotion. I want to be clear that emotion and passion are not the same thing: I'm not suggesting we need to become calloused and hardened to the problem we're trying to solve. That would help no one. The end goal is not to create data-driven robots who no longer feel the weight of the issue, but we can still feel deeply passionate and also not base our decisions on emotion.

Finally, this deep dive is going to teach us who the major players are when it comes to this topic and our idea. Chances are very, very high there is someone, somewhere out in the world who is doing or has done something at least tangentially related to what we would like to do. Even if our big idea is completely fresh and innovative, it is still almost certainly a cross between a few other ideas/realities.

This deep dive will help us begin to understand who the major players are in our "space." We don't want this list so that we know our "competitors," by the way. We want this list so that we can know whom we might be able to learn from, partner with, and enter into collaboration alongside. This is the number-one vetting question I use when people approach me with the idea of starting a new nonprofit (which happens several times a year). I always say something to the effect of "This sounds like a great idea. Can you do some research and come back and share with me who else in the world is doing something similar and how you might partner with them or differentiate yourself from them significantly?" More than half of the people never reach back out to me to answer that question, a fact that always baffles me, as I don't believe that bar is very high at all.

Once we've done our deep dive and walked all the way around our problem/solution/big idea, it's time to get to work.

> Once we've done our deep dive and walked all the way around our problem/solution/big idea, it's time to get to work.

This next portion of our discussion is going to assume that we did not discover others already doing what we would like to do. If we did, we should reach out to them and see if there is a mutually beneficial way we can partner or collaborate. In the absolute worst case, they'll decline. Over the years, I have reached out to dozens of businesses, ministries, nonprofits, and even just individual people who were a few steps ahead of me when it came to whatever big problem I was trying to solve. I have never had someone outright turn me down from at least asking them a few key questions. We didn't always end up working together, but I always learned something from them that made the rest of my journey both smoother and more successful.

But let's assume you haven't found anyone doing what you want to do or you've fully leveraged what you can from those you found doing similar work. Now it's time to move from having many data pieces about an idea to actually creating something. The next step is to actually take a step. To borrow from others before me like Elisabeth Elliot, Mother Teresa, and even *The Big Book* of AA, our next step is to "Do the next right thing. Then do it again." In our case, the next right thing is the first big step of bringing our idea to life.

Let's walk through this together:

1. Grab a blank piece of paper and a pencil (or use a laptop or your computer if you prefer).
2. Write your big idea at the top of the page. (What is it that you're hoping to accomplish?)
3. Now at the bottom of the page, with plenty of white space between, write down what will change if you accomplish your big idea. This is a reminder for you of what is at stake.

Here's what mine would have looked like for Mercy Project:

---

**Big Idea:** Rescue Children from Human Trafficking in Ghana, Africa

**Outcome:** Many Children Are Reunited Back with Their Families and Attend School

---

That's all I started with 10 years ago. Seriously. There was not a single thing more formal or fancy or process driven than that. I had an idea (rescue children from human trafficking in Ghana, Africa), and I knew what the outcome would be if my idea worked (children are reunited back with their families and attend school).

Now go back up to just below your big idea and answer one simple but crucial question: Why does this matter to me?

This is your "why," and you can go read Simon Sinek's important work *Start with Why* if you want a whole book on starting with or finding your why. But let me make it as simple as possible. You need to ask yourself, Why do I care? That's the North Star of your big idea.

Your why keeps you motivated, inspired, and persisting when bringing your big idea to life becomes hard.

Your why keeps you motivated, inspired, and persisting when bringing your big idea to life becomes hard. And if what you're trying to do matters, if what you're seeking to accomplish makes a difference, if it is not just another idea but a great idea, then you will absolutely meet resistance. You'll meet resistance because you'll make other people nervous, and when we make other people feel nervous, they lash out. So this *why* sentence just below your big idea is your life jacket when you feel like you're drowning in the future sea of uncertainty.

Here's what my big idea page would have looked like once I added my why statement:

**Big Idea:** Rescue Children from Human Trafficking in Ghana, Africa

**Why:** I want to give my life to something bigger. I want to tangibly respond when I see injustice. I want my children to see justice and mercy are actions, not just words.

**Outcome:** Many Children Are Reunited Back with Their Families and Attend School

So now we have our big idea, our why, and the result of what will come to life once we see our big ideas through.

Now comes the fun, hard, and beautiful part. The part that separates those who have big ideas and those who achieve big ideas. The part that changes someone from a dreamer to a doer. This next part is where people with lots of ideas but little follow-through get stuck and bogged down. We have to commit to not allowing that to happen to us, which is exactly why we're walking through this activity together.

This is where we list out the steps that need to take place for us to turn our idea into reality. Use a pencil here because some of what we write will be erased, combined into other steps, or at the very least reordered. Don't worry about the sequence of your steps right now. We can arrange them chronologically later. The worst decision we can make is to spend a disproportionate amount of time trying to decide where to start.

Here are some action steps I would have written down for Mercy Project:

- Get 501c3 approval from the IRS.
- Open a bank account.
- Find someone to create a logo.
- Start social media pages.
- Build a website.
- Raise money.
- Go back to Ghana to find possible partnerships with local nonprofits.

Okay, a lot of people—*a lot* of people—would've kept that list in their head because it felt too stressful to lay it all out on paper. Others would've put it down on paper and then walked away, trying to catch their breath, because seeing it all written out overwhelmed them. But it doesn't have to be that way!

Let's look at my list again so I can walk you through exactly what I did to accomplish each one of these action steps:

- Get 501c3 approval from the IRS—I Googled, found, and hired a company out of Atlanta that specializes in doing this. For a fee of $500, they saved me a week of frustrating paperwork. Total time spent: 4 hours.

- Open a bank account—I drove to the bank with my IRS paperwork and asked for an account. Total time spent: 1 hour.
- Find someone to create a logo—I called and asked my favorite graphic designer friend, Gretchen, to do this for us. (A year later, I hired her to work for Mercy Project.) Total time spent: 10 minutes.
- Start social media pages—I sat down and did it. Total time spent: 1 hour
- Build a website—I asked my much-savvier-than-me brother and a few friends to help me "build my own website." I hated every minute of it. Total time spent: 15–20 hours.
- Raise money—This was a bigger step that needed to be broken down into more steps. Total time spent: 2 hours (to plan my next fundraising steps).
    1. Ask people to make monthly gifts.
    2. Ask people for more substantial one-time gifts.
    3. Start a local 5K Turkey Trot.
    4. Invite friends to participate in a world record attempt to raise money and awareness.
- Go back to Ghana to find possible partnerships with local nonprofits—This also needed to be broken down further. First, I needed to find room in my schedule; then book a flight; then make an itinerary to make the most of my time in Africa; then reach out to potential nonprofits with requests to meet. Total time: 10–15 hours.

I hope you'll forgive me if that sort of detail is not helpful to you, but I took the time to create that plan and then made the decision to include it here for two reasons. First, what seemed like an overwhelming to-do list only took me about 40 hours to complete—one week's worth of work. Even if this was a side gig, which it was for me for the first year after my trip to Ghana, you could accomplish all of this over just a few months' time if you were intentional with your 14-minute blocks of good. Second, I wanted to show you how we typically overthink, overanalyze, over-everything when it comes to big ideas. I know people (and you do too) who would have spent 40 hours just trying to decide which bank they should approach to start an account. If we multiply that kind of decision times the hundreds we'll have to make to execute our plan, it's very easy to see how we could become overwhelmed and eventually abandon our big idea completely.

Could I have done some of those steps better or at a lower cost? Probably. Was the very small amount of money I might have saved worth tens or even a collective hundred hours of my time? Absolutely not.

My local bank and social media pages and even the self-designed website could all be changed (and all have been multiple times in the past 10 years, by the way), but the other steps carried more weight because there was no room for error in achieving my 501c3 status from the IRS, raising enough money to put our plan in action, and establishing the right partnerships in Ghana so we could actually solve the problem. Those items took up the bulk of my time and energy, and the rest still got done.

If this process seems too easy—well, then, you're welcome. There are no tricks or hidden steps. It really is just a matter of making a to-do list and then doing it. One next right thing at a time. One day at a time. One compassionate, courageous, and creative act at a time.

Of course, your list will evolve as your project does. Some items will only need to be done once (like filing for your nonprofit status with the IRS), some will need to be done every few years (we've built 3 websites in 10 years), and some will stay on permanently (fundraising), but the who/what/when/where will change in time. As your project grows, you grow too. You learn, adapt, make new relationships, find new problems, and create new solutions, all while remaining passionate and committed to the original *why* that sparked you into action from the start.

The list I detailed here was my first list for Mercy Project, but it was certainly not my last. The list changes, the organization changes, some of the ideas change, but the way we go about executing those things pretty much stays the same. List them out, break them down by actionable next steps, and get them done. Wash, rinse, repeat. Some items take years; others take seconds. Prioritize, make sure they're aligned with your North Star, roll up your sleeves, and get to work.

> The world is not changed with just great ideas or good intentions. It's changed by people who persist in turning big ideas into actionable steps.

The world is not changed with just great ideas or good intentions. It's changed by people who persist in turning big ideas into actionable steps. Persistence is the way we change the world. Show up. Stick around. Persist until you achieve transformation. This is how big ideas become manageable. This is how big ideas turn into real solutions. This is how dreams put on shoes and start walking around to make a true difference in the lives of other people—14 minutes at a time.

Getting our big ideas out into the world can feel a lot like hard work. But we don't have to do this alone. In fact, we were never supposed to. We're better together. But how do we get people on board with our big ideas so that our 14 minutes a day become exponentially impactful, beyond what we can even imagine? It's not as difficult as you may think.

# CHAPTER TWENTY

# Getting People to Join Your Big Idea

This chapter turns to examine the second part of the equation when it comes to fostering creativity and executing of big ideas: "I want to know how to share my creative visions with others and get them on board instead of immediately dismissing them as too far-fetched."

Maybe you've personally wondered about this. If so, good news: This chapter is going to be as direct and straightforward as the last one, with real, tangible, actionable steps for how I and others like me have encouraged people to back our big ideas. Not once, not twice, but over and over again. This is the exact same system and process you can start using for your next big idea and all the ones to come after that.

I am convinced that many people are looking for leaders to follow—and you can be that leader. Yes, you! Many people do not want to be the ones coming up with big ideas, or they are not gifted at dreaming up big ideas, or they are afraid to put themselves out there, so they are looking around, just hungry for someone to come along and confidently say, "This is where we are going. I need your help. Let's go there together."

Time and again, I find people incredibly agreeable to jumping in on a big idea if the vision is cast well and by someone they trust. When I put myself out there as a trustworthy leader who will follow through with a plan and I cast a vision that feels exciting and meaningful, people will get on board. I could tell you a hundred stories of this happening in my own life—from small moments to grand projects that stretched across the world.

One of my favorites is when I started a marathon in my hometown. As I'm writing this book, we're making plans for our tenth-annual edition of this race, and the event has not only hosted more than 40,000 runners over its first decade but also has raised more than a million dollars to local children's charities, including Mercy Project. It's easy to look back now and realize that starting the marathon was a great idea, but this wasn't always so apparent. The idea of holding the event was met with a fair amount of resistance and numerous naysayers from the very beginning, especially when I told people I wanted to hold the first one just seven months after the idea's inception. Here's how it all came about.

I am a runner, and my dad was a runner, so one of the first official fundraisers Mercy Project hosted was a Turkey Trot in my hometown of College Station, Texas. It was a very low-budget event with no chip timing. My 75 year old grandmother literally stood at the finish line passing out numbered popsicle sticks to finishers so we could keep track of finishing places. The winner received a frozen turkey donated by the local grocery store! But the race was a success, and we made some money for Mercy Project.

A few months later, I saw someone post on a local message board, asking why our town didn't have a marathon, and I immediately thought, "Hey, I organized a 5K. I should start a marathon. That would be awesome."

Fast-forward just a month or so later when 27-year-old Chris (a young man no one knows and one who has zero credibility in town) walks into a city government building surrounded by various employees, traffic-control engineers, and other important people who were all there at my request to talk about what it would take to start a marathon. In the room were representatives of two different cities, Texas A&M University, and the Texas Department of Transportation. They would all have to agree to the event if it was going to happen because the race would affect each of them significantly. I had no idea what I was doing, and I am grateful that ignorance is bliss because I stood there with certainty and announced, "Our town needs a marathon. It's going to be a lot of hard work, and it's going to require a partnership between the two cities the race would run through and Texas A&M, but I know we can do it. Let's do something great together."

To my amazement, they said yes.

In preparation for writing this chapter, I reached out to one of the key stakeholders who had attended that meeting (and has since become a friend of mine), asking what she remembered about that first impression. She responded: "You had two things going for you when leading that meeting: passion and a plan. Doing large events, I know it can be difficult to get people to the same chapter, much less the same page, quickly. When I got back to my office that day, my staff asked me if I thought the event would actually happen. I told them that day, 'It's happening.'"

> A leader is someone with passion and a plan.
> Indeed, that is all it takes to be a leader. That's
> the kind of person others will line up to follow.

I should send my friend a bouquet of flowers for gifting me such a simple new definition for leadership. A leader is someone with passion and a plan. Indeed, that is all it takes to be a leader. That's the kind of person others will line up to follow.

Speaking of a plan, this is the second way we inspire people to join us in executing our big ideas. We show them we have a viable plan. This serves two major purposes. First, most people are not visionaries, so they need to see there is a clear and well-thought-out path to get where you say you need them to go. Some people might trust you enough for you just to say, "Hey, we're going somewhere and you should come with me!" but most people do not fall into that category. The vast majority are going to want to see you have a plan. It doesn't have to be perfect, and it doesn't have to be final. But they want to see that you have thought through some of the potential challenges and obstacles. This goes back to the value of the deep dive we talked about in the previous chapter. When I walked into that room with city officials, I knew more than they did about marathons being hosted in other cities. I had arrived well prepared to serve as the expert in the room when it came to the specific topic of marathons in Texas. I also presented a plan. Now it probably got thrown out the window as soon as we all started talking and I realized how much I didn't know I didn't know, but that's not what they saw. They saw I had a plan. I came prepared to cast a vision, establish myself as an expert, and show them a plan of the action steps I believed it would take for us to achieve our goal and launch a marathon.

The second purpose that having a plan serves is that it shows people you are committed and willing to suffer and do hard things to see your idea come to life. As Rachel Hollis once said (and I agree with this 100 percent), "No one will ever care about your dream as much as you do." We cannot walk into a meeting with key stakeholders and potential partners and casually suggest, "Hey, you guys want to start a marathon?" The answer will most certainly be, "No." They clearly don't want to start a marathon, because if that's what they wanted, they would have done so already. What they are willing to do is listen to someone who *does* want to start a marathon, someone who is willing to sacrifice to make the marathon happen, someone who can cast a vision that allows them to fill in the blanks with their own respective gifts and talents. They could get behind that, even if they'd never care about the marathon as much as I did.

Here is what I tell people all the time about their big idea/ dream/new business: However much you care about this new thing, your very biggest fans are going to be a few notches below that. So on a scale of 1 to 10, with 10 being the absolute highest possible passion and buy-in for a big idea, if you're an 8, your biggest fans will be 6s and the people who merely like you will be 4s. This is why you need to be a 12 (again, on a scale of 1 to 10) when it comes to how much you personally care and are willing to sacrifice to see your dream come to life. If you won't show up early, stay up late, eat, drink, and breathe the plan to get it off the ground, neither will anyone else (and neither *should* anyone else). Having a plan shows people that you're putting your time and money where your mouth is, so to speak. This is huge. Confidently casting a vision with a plan you're willing to sacrifice to achieve is critical in getting others to support your big idea. But there are other ways to ensure your success as well.

Do not underestimate the power of momentum. People like to win. It's part of our competitive human nature. If people are choosing one of two ideas to give themselves to, and all other things are equal, they will usually choose the one they believe has the best chance of working. Who can blame them? No one wants to pour ourselves into something that we don't believe will ultimately work. And if it does fail, well . . . that's a terrible feeling *but* it's also an opportunity to learn and grow and do better next time.

Here's a fascinating piece of data to reinforce the idea that people like to be a part of things that work. Many of you are probably familiar with Kickstarter, the massive crowdsourcing platform. Kickstarter allows someone to create an online fundraising campaign and invite others to invest in their ideas. These investors are called backers, and they usually receive some level of perks that scales with their donation. Kickstarter has been outrageously successful, helping to fund more than 200,000 projects to the tune of more than $5 billion. Yes, *billion* with a *B*.

> Kickstarter campaigns that reach just 20 percent of their goal will go on to reach 100 percent 4 out of 5 times. Those are great odds. That's the power of momentum.

Kickstarter is unique in that it operates on an "all or nothing" basis. That is, if you don't raise 100 percent or more of your goal, then your backers are not charged and you get nothing. Here's how this applies to you, whether you ever start a Kickstarter campaign or not: Kickstarter campaigns that reach just 20 percent of their goal will go on to reach 100 percent 4 out of 5 times. Those are great odds. That's the power of momentum.[1] Many, many people don't want to be the first to jump in, but they are willing to jump in early if they see momentum. This is illustrated clearly in these Kickstarter statistics, and the same will be true for us as we share our big ideas with others and get them on board.

I once had a financial donor for a new project tell me, "I don't want to be your first donation on this one. But come back to me when you're close, and I'll gladly be the last one." He was politely saying, "I don't know if this will work. But if it does—I'm in."

People may not communicate that message to us as clearly as that donor did to me, but I can promise you they are thinking and feeling it, even if they don't know exactly how to articulate it. So how do we gain momentum before we go and ask people to join us? Isn't that a bit of a chicken and an egg scenario? Not really.

The first way to gain momentum involves much of what I've noted previously, so I won't belabor this discussion here. Be sure to have a plan and vision, and establish yourself as an expert. After you've done that, start with the people who have the most to gain from your creative idea. The ones who will share in your win in some capacity. People who will benefit or "look good" when your idea works.

> Be sure to have a plan and vision, and establish yourself as an expert. After you've done that, start with the people who have the most to gain from your creative idea.

Now I know some people might think the part about finding people who will "look good" when your idea works might consider that to be some sort of political game of deceitfulness or pandering to vanity, but that is really not the point at all. There are potential allies who will benefit if your project succeeds—some of them by default. Think of a principal if a teacher has a creative idea, or a midlevel manager if someone in their department has a creative idea, or an executive director if someone in their nonprofit has a creative idea. Whoever will win "with you" if your idea works should be the easiest person to first get onboard with your idea. As long as you present it well.

Let's start with what not to do when it comes to that initial pitch.

Imagine a guy runs up to you. He's sweating and flushed with excitement. "Hey," he says. "I had this big, crazy, audacious idea, and I've created a plan for it and everything. Can I tell you about it and see what you think?"

You'll probably feel a little worried that he's about to ask you for help. You're probably too busy to take on another responsibility, and you're already stretched too thin. You're probably wondering how you can politely end this conversation and get back to your already-packed to-do list. That's probably what you're thinking, regardless of how you actually respond.

But what if someone approached you like this instead: "Hey, I've been working on a new idea for a project that I think could be a big win for us. I don't necessarily need your help on it because I know you're busy, but I would love your feedback on how I can execute it in a way that makes the greatest impact. Can we set up a meeting for just 15 to 20 minutes so I can share it with you?"

What key differences do you notice between these two approaches? Read them again carefully. Here is what makes the second example so much more compelling than the first:

First, he doesn't use words like *crazy* and *audacious*. Those are scary.

Second, he emphasizes the shared value of his idea: "This could be a big win for us."

Third, he makes it clear that he will take sole ownership of the project. It won't fall on you.

Fourth, he asks for your feedback. This honors your intelligence and expertise by saying, "I need you," but in a time-sensitive way.

Fifth, he's not asking for permission—he's asking for your feedback so he can make the greatest impact. Huge difference.

Finally, he honors your time by setting up an appointment to discuss the next steps. This is beneficial to him because the hallway, break room, or parking lot is not conducive to getting you on board.

Okay, so now you know how *you* should approach someone with your big idea. (It's always helpful to step into their shoes first and imagine how they feel.)

Now that you've politely and respectfully approached a potential partner or mentor, and they've agreed to meet with you for 10 to 15 minutes to offer feedback about your big idea, what should you do now that it's time for the actual meeting? Do not, I repeat, do not pull out your 16-page single-spaced plan and lay it on their desk. I am begging you—they will want to crawl under their desk and disappear. Instead, give them a high-level summary. This should be done in 5 minutes tops. If you can't say it in 5 minutes or less, you're not ready for the meeting.

Once you have shared a very cohesive, very clear, very concise high-level summary, ask specific questions you've prepared for them. Not "What do you think?" but "How do you think HR will want to handle this?" or "Do you think this is something the church will get excited about?" or "Do you see how this will be valuable to our customers?"

Then the hard part comes. We have to be quiet and listen.

Remember, they are hearing this for the first time. They have not thought and prayed about, studied, and dissected this idea in a hundred different ways like you have. Because you've spent so much time thinking about this idea, it is likely you have already considered most anything they might initially say to you. That's good! In fact, it should be the goal. It means you asked the right questions when you did your deep dive. But now is not the time to interrupt them or give a counterpoint to every statement they make. Listen, write it all down, and honor their feedback.

When they are done, you can say something like, "I'm so excited to hear you share those concerns because those are some of the same concerns I originally had and the ones I've spent the most time solving so that we can ensure this is a success. I've outlined them all in the plan I put together, and I would love to share that with you in more detail, if that would be helpful."

Can you feel how different this is compared with how these meetings usually go? Do you see now why taking a deep dive, preparing, and making ourselves an expert is so critical? This is what I mean when I talk about gaining momentum. This is the prework that gets you ready for the meeting. In turn, your preparation will give you a much higher chance of success. Here is the enduring message you want the person in that meeting to hear: "I have an idea. It will be good for both of us. I will own it. You can help me make it better and more successful if you'd like." That's it. Almost no one says no to a new idea when presented like that.

> "I have an idea. It will be good for both of us. I will own it. You can help make it better and more successful if you'd like."

What I outlined here feels more like an interaction between a manager and an employee, but it works exactly the same with colleagues, friends, and community leaders. Tattoo these words into your mind when trying to get people on board with a new idea: "I have an idea. It will be good for both of us. I will own it. You can help make it better and more successful if you'd like."

You can call it *IWOO* for short:

1. My **I**dea
2. We **W**in
3. My **O**wnership
4. Your **O**ption

If you are committed to making things happen, tattoo (or at least write down) those four letters (IWOO) somewhere important. Because you will come back to them time and again. There are no real shortcuts or secret sauces when it comes to turning big ideas into reality, but IWOO is about as close as it comes to having one. Memorize it, practice it, and execute it. You will find it is incredibly valuable in the process of creating allies and partners to help you launch your big ideas.

The final part that is critically important here is being able to communicate what exactly it is you need from the people who say they are willing to help. Don't waste the opportunity and momentum when someone says, "I love it. Let's do it. What's next?" by not being able to answer that question.

What was it about them that made you choose to approach them in the first place? Did you need their permission? Do you need their affirmation to give you confidence? Do you need their money? Their time? A certain skill they possess? The reason you want them to be involved should be made clear here. "You can help me by [fill in the blank]."

If the answer is, "I am not exactly sure yet; I just knew I had to get you involved one way or another," then great. Own that. Communicate that. Tell them you'll be back in touch within a firm time frame, and then be sure to actually follow up when you said you would. I never cease to be amazed by the number of great plans that are spoiled simply because of a lack of follow-through. Don't let your big idea die in the graveyard of good intentions.

> Don't let your big idea die in the graveyard of good intentions.

This is how you gain momentum. By the way, when people start saying "yes" to being involved, you can be sure and mention those "yes" responses to the next people you talk to. Call it the Kickstarter effect. As I've pointed out, lots of people don't want to be the first, but most people are happy to join in, and are even motivated by a fear of missing out, once they believe something is actually going to happen. So share those previous wins with the people you meet with next, and start stacking those wins on top of each other.

I will end this chapter by echoing what I said in the last paragraph of the previous chapter: Getting our big ideas out into the world can feel a lot like hard work. Part of that hard work is building momentum, one person at a time. By building that momentum, we will reach the point where all the pieces fall into place. At that point, we'll have created the right idea, the right plan, and even the right team to bring it all to life. This is when the fun begins!

## NOTE

[1]"Stats," Kickstarter, www.kickstarter.com/help/stats.

# CHAPTER TWENTY-ONE

# Amplification

Early on in this book, I talked about the power of compounding good that comes when we make small decisions every single day that add up to massive change after days, weeks, months, and years. This is how just 14 minutes a day becomes nearly 2 hours a week, which becomes 8 hours a month, which becomes 100 hours a year, and eventually 2,000 to 3,000 hours over a working career. I mentioned this before, and I believe it bears repeating here: We continue to massively underestimate the potential impact of small decisions made every day while at the same time overestimating the impact of these "once in a decade" type moments that are honestly more a product of luck or being in the right place at the right time than they are anything else. If this was the single truth from this book that took root in you, then I'd feel like I've done my job. But there's another kind of amplification that bears mentioning here too.

> We continue to massively underestimate the potential impact of small decisions made every day while at the same time overestimating the impact of these "once in a decade" type moments that are honestly more a product of luck or being in the right place at the right time than they are anything else.

When I came home from that first trip to Ghana so many years ago and Stacey and I sent out letters and homemade DVDs to many of our friends and family, inviting them to help us help the children in Ghana, there were a number of generous people who responded positively to our initiative. But there was one response that changed the course of my life forever, and possibly may change yours too, since you're reading this book.

Stacey had a cousin named Ronda who was married to a man named Dean. I had met both Dean and Ronda before (at our wedding several years earlier), but we certainly didn't know each other well. But something about our letter and very amateur DVD really resonated with Dean and Ronda in a way that we could have never expected. They made a generous financial donation that we will always be grateful for, but they did more than that. Dean called me one day and asked me a bunch of questions about what I had seen and experienced in Ghana, and then he asked if they could travel there with me sometime.

Now, remember, I had only been to Ghana once at this point, and I was still working full time at a different job. This was before the idea of starting Mercy Project was even on our radar. So I politely let Dean know that I would be happy to take them to Ghana sometime, but I didn't feel like an adequate or capable tour guide. He was undeterred, and just a few months later, the three of us were all on a Delta Airlines flight together to Ghana.

It was on that trip, sitting around a wobbly plastic table and eating chicken and rice (again), that Dean and Ronda challenged me to use my newfound passion and gifts to do more than help the children in Ghana as a side gig or hobby. They asked me point blank what scared me the most about giving more of myself to the work in Ghana. I told them it was fear about providing for my family (our daughter Micah was about four months old at this point), and they told me they would help ensure that finances were not a concern if I felt like this is what I needed to be doing.

Now I could stop the story here, and you might think it was wonderful that Dean and Ronda chose to be so generous. And it's true—Mercy Project would have likely never started if it were not for their initial generosity and gentle prodding for me to go for it. But the amazing fact is that their financial generosity might have been the least impactful part of our entire relationship.

From that trip all the way to the present day, Dean and Ronda have poured into me personally and professionally in ways I could never fully explain or express. They have been my biggest cheerleaders, my most honest truth tellers, my wisest counsel, and my "we will be right here behind you no matter what happens" people. You see, Dean is a business consultant who has spent a career helping solve some of the most complex problems in some of the largest companies in the world. Saying he is excellent at what he does would be an understatement. He is extraordinarily talented. This has given him a number of incredible opportunities throughout his career and also allowed him to promise young dreamers like me that he could help with the financial part if I would take the leap of faith on the showing up part.

But here's what I don't want you to miss. Dean used his very best gifts of mentorship, problem solving, and creativity not to solve a single problem or two during his spare time but to pour into me so that I could solve hard problems full time. Dean gave his 14 minutes a day to me, day after day, week after week, month after month, and year after year. In doing so, Dean and Ronda's fingerprints are all over every single good thing I've ever done since then. This is the immeasurable power of amplification. This is why if you flip back to page seven of this book, you'll see I dedicated it to Dean and his intentional and relentless gift of pouring into me 14 minutes at a time.

Hundreds of formerly enslaved children in Ghana are now free because of Dean's investment in Mercy Project and his belief in me. By dedicating his time to traveling to Africa, learning about the problem, and directing his resources to helping me solve the problem through Mercy Project, thousands of people across Ghana now have a better way of fishing and earning a sustainable income. Now, when I have the chance to speak across the country or write books like this one, Dean's voice and gift of time to me are amplified over and over again—even if the audience never knows it. This is the immeasurable power of amplification.

> Can you imagine the collective impact if every single seasoned person in the world took a 20-something-year-old under their wing and gave them 14 minutes a day of hard-earned lessons and wisdom?

There might be no greater use of our 14 minutes a day than to pour ourselves not just into projects that matter the most to us, but also into the people who can give their time and attention to making sure those projects succeed. Can you imagine the collective impact if every single seasoned person in the world took a 20-something-year-old under their wing and gave them 14 minutes a day of hard-earned lessons and wisdom? Could we even calculate the collective positive influence if every single aspiring and passionate but "wet behind the ears" nonprofit leader had a Dean in their lives to help them solve some of their most pressing challenges faster, more efficiently, and with the kind of sustainability that only comes from a lifetime of learning things the hard way?

When we pour into those coming up behind us, the compounding effect from that amplification is truly infinite. There is absolutely no way to ever measure the impact of Dean's willingness to invest his time in me. It's immeasurable because I turn and invest it into other people, who invest it into other people, who invest it into . . . I think you get the point. Suffice it to say generations of people are impacted when we share our very best gifts in the way Dean chose to share his with me. This is why I hope every single one of us will consider using part or all of our 14 minutes of good each day not to simply do our own good, but to help equip someone else along the way to do the same. This is the immeasurable power of amplification when it comes to doing good.

# CHAPTER TWENTY-TWO

# Inspiration

Before we wrap this up, I want to share a handful of stories that I believe will inspire and empower you to take what we've talked about throughout this book and create a true impact in your own life—14 minutes at a time. That is really the point of every page you've read so far, and I will honestly consider my job incomplete if something you've ingested along the way doesn't plant a seed in you that produces compassionate, courageous, and creative fruit to go out and do more good for others.

Each one of these stories I share here is worthy of taking up an entire chapter of this book, but for the sake of efficiency and because I know we all connect with different stories for different reasons, I'm going to share them with you in a summarized format, rather than as long-form narratives.

The main characters in each of these stories are ordinary people like you and me—people who allowed themselves to feel compassion, found their courage, and turned their big ideas into actionable solutions for real problems.

> The main characters in each of these stories are ordinary people like you and me—people who allowed themselves to feel compassion, found their courage, and turned their big ideas into actionable solutions for real problems.

Your task is to find yourself in each one of these stories. To find the places where you share their compassion, courage, and creativity and then use those connecting points to empower you to believe that you too are capable of these same possibilities in your own life.

I also want you to find the places where you don't share their compassion, courage, and creativity. Use those moments as reflection opportunities:

1. What is it they did that scares you?
2. What keeps you from making the kind of decisions they made?
3. Are those objections and limitations legitimate or self-imposed?
4. Can you distinguish between not wanting to do something and not being willing to do what it takes to do something?
5. Why does that feel so hard for us to own sometimes?

Some of these stories led to big, giant, breakthrough moments that changed the world. These cases obviously took years of persistence and consistency. But they were built one day at a time. One choice at a time. One "next right thing" at a time. Often 14 minutes at a time.

Other stories shared here explore a situation that lasted only a moment. A brief spark of someone daring to choose courage, compassion, and creativity. A choice that benefitted both parties and potentially started a domino effect whose lasting impact we will almost certainly never know.

But all the stories of real change here share one common thread: They can be our story if we choose. Because compassion, courage, and creativity are a choice each one of us has the chance to make every single day, and when combined, they have the explosive power to change not only ourselves but the world around us.

> Because compassion, courage, and creativity are a choice each one of us has the chance to make every single day, and when combined, they have the explosive power to change not only ourselves but the world around us.

I have a friend named Shelby who is a teacher. In her first year of teaching life skills to students with significant cognitive impairments and adaptive disabilities at a high school just outside Houston, she came up with the brilliant idea of wanting to empower her students in some way that was meaningful and would outlast their time with her in the classroom.

So she purchased all the things they would need to start a traveling coffee cart. This would allow her students to walk around to the school staff members, take their orders, and then deliver their coffee to them on Fridays. Most importantly, this would allow the students to practice their social and communication skills, working through their shyness and even learning how to run a simple business by calculating their expenses and profits. They named their business "The Grizzly Bean."

I was so impressed when I heard what Shelby was doing that I immediately reached out to her for more information. It was obvious that her heart behind this was *enormous* and pure. Not only was she putting a lot of her time and energy into this, but she was also self-funding the whole thing on a first-year teacher's salary. We quickly made sure she was made whole on that front and encouraged her to keep dreaming big.

One of the coolest parts of this story is that Shelby has the goal of using some of the profits from her class's coffee business to provide funds for another school to start the same project. Then they would do the same, and they would do the same, and so on and so forth. How cool is that?

I shared Shelby's story on my Facebook page a few years ago. Consequently, it was shared more than 28,000 times, which resulted in media coverage by Houston news stations, *Parents* magazine, and Yahoo!, among many other outlets. Many of the nearly 500 comments on the original post were from teachers who'd felt inspired to start something similar in their school after reading Shelby's story. The domino effect lives on!

～

When our son Lincoln turned 4 years old, we told him he could choose any restaurant in town for his birthday lunch. He was unwavering in his request: Whataburger. God bless Texas.

Shout-out to the general manager and staff who overheard it was Lincoln's birthday and brought out a warm cinnamon roll and sang him Happy Birthday with much gusto. That may be a first for them, but they owned it and our kiddo loved it. Can doing a little bit of good for others be this simple? Yes, it can. It certainly was that memorable day.

～

In 2019, I shared a story on my Facebook page about a single mother with five young children who needed a new place to live.

Her current situation was not just less than ideal (six people in two bedrooms) but was frankly bordering on criminal, as her landlord regularly tried to engage her inappropriately for rent reductions. She was tired of it and turned to me for help.

A day or two after I posted about her situation, I got an email from a couple in San Antonio. They asked me to call them because they had an idea. I was intrigued and reached out.

Now, to be clear, I hardly knew this couple. They followed me on Facebook, donated regularly to Mercy Project, and ran in our marathon most years. But it would've been a stretch to call them my friends. At least before that phone call.

When I called, they told me they were moved by the story of the single mom and wanted to be people of action. They asked if I would help them find a suitable house in College Station that they could buy for the purpose of renting to her at an affordable rate. I was shocked. Floored. Blessed. Humbled. Challenged. I explained to them that the maximum rent she could afford would likely not be enough to cover their monthly expenses, which meant they would be operating at a loss every month. They said they knew that and believed this was the right thing to do, regardless of the numbers. Incredible. The young mom moved into the house they bought just a few months later.

Police officer Damon Cole uses his time off-duty to visit terminally ill children while dressed as Superman, Batman, and the Incredible Hulk, among others. One article said he's traveled to nearly a dozen states, including an 11-hour drive to see a terminally ill child and a 5-hour trip to make a midnight appearance for a boy approaching death. Do you have the ability to dress up as a superhero and visit hospitals? Of course you do. I do too.

Bea Gaddy lived in Baltimore, where she would sometimes have to rummage through the trash to find what she needed to survive. In 1981, she purchased a lottery ticket for 50 cents and won $290. She used the money to feed a Thanksgiving meal to nearly 40 struggling people. This began a new tradition in which Gaddy, supported by donations and volunteers, would feed the hungry every Thanksgiving. By Thanksgiving Day 1991, 10 years after her first "Thanks for Giving" feast, she was leading an enormous team of volunteers that would feed 17,000 people across the city. Referred to as Baltimore's Mother Teresa, Gaddy would continue her Thanksgiving tradition every year for 30 years until she eventually passed away from breast cancer. Gaddy had a vision she was willing to sacrifice for, and people followed her because of it.

Simple stories. Profoundly powerful. Achievable by almost all of us. If only we will allow ourselves to be compassionate, courageous, and creative, these can be our stories too.

# CHAPTER TWENTY-THREE

# Turning Your
# Compassion, Courage,
# and Creativity
# into Good

To close out our time together, I want to go all the way back to Connor's story from Chapter One. The tools and sources of inspiration you've been presented with throughout this book are the same ones that led Connor to realize he was capable of significantly more impact than he'd previously imagined. These tools helped Connor understand his opportunity for impact was here and now, rather than some-time down the road or when [fill in the blank] happened.

But I still think many of us read stories about others doing good, even stories like Connor's, and internally determine that these situations or circumstances are different from our own or that the individuals involved are somehow more qualified or have skills and talents that lend themselves to more obvious opportunities for doing good. Again, forgive my frankness, but that's a lie we tell ourselves—an excuse to let ourselves off the hook from doing what each of us is fully capable of doing. To that end, I want to share a bullet point list of the types of opportunities that exist for people with various skills, talents, passions, and time to do more good just 14 minutes at a time.

> If I spent 5 minutes with any single one of you sharing some of your interests, talents, and passions with me, I could name at least 5 ways you could leverage your 14 minutes a day to do more good in the world.

I hesitate to even start a list like this because those who don't find themselves on the list (which could never be exhaustive because the possibilities are truly infinite) might feel even more sure that this billion hours of good movement is somehow beyond them. So let me say this: If I spent 5 minutes with any single one of you sharing some of your interests, talents, and passions with me, I could name at least 5 ways you could leverage your 14 minutes a day to do more good in the world. That has nothing to do with me and everything to do with you. I don't even need to know you to know that you are capable of so much more good than you could possibly ever imagine. So if you don't happen to find yourself anywhere on the following list, look again—both here on this list and out there in the world around you.

- Are you good at car repairs? There are single moms all over your town who know nothing about cars and who may not have the finances to tackle routine vehicle maintenance. Find them, help them, and teach them. The same could be done for home maintenance, personal finance, cooking, gardening, and a host of other things as well.
- Are you a teacher or tutor? Use your skills to help adults with reading difficulties or for whom passing the GED would be life changing. Find the most annoying kid in the class (yep, that was me) and pour into them with

everything you have. Support families who struggle to support their children's educational journey. (You are saints, by the way.)

- Are you good at accounting or finance? Someone needs you to help them read a balance sheet and P&L. Someone may be trying to head a nonprofit or childcare service without any business experience or training. When I started Mercy Project, for the first year, I literally kept the "books" in a Microsoft Word document. I truly wish I was kidding. Do you know what I would have done for someone to help me set up a real accounting system, even in an Excel document? My story is not unique. Find someone and help them.

- Are you good at saving and budgeting? You are surrounded by people who lack that knowledge. Share your budget. Share your tricks and tips. Mentor them. The skills you transfer could give them the financial means to pay off debt, start a college fund, and change the story for many generations to come.

- Are you a business owner? Take the service your business provides (whether it's making delicious food, selling mattresses, offering computer repair, etc.) and find people who need that gift. Create partnerships with the organizations serving the people who could benefit most from your services. Hospital employees know which families can't afford food, social workers know which families have kids sleeping on the floor, and Boys and Girls Clubs have computers gathering dust that they can't afford to get repaired.

- Are you good at sales? Who could really, really benefit from your product but never afford it? How could you help a nonprofit refine its sales pitch to be more compelling? How could you volunteer to teach a class on persuasion—an invaluable skill that each one of us uses in life every single day?

- Are you a stay-at-home parent? What did you do before you stayed at home? You certainly haven't lost that skill. How could you leverage your flexibility to help those who don't have it? Picking up prescriptions for older neighbors, cooking an extra serving of dinner for the friend whose partner travels often for work, being available to take the forgotten project to school for the parent who would have to clock out and possibly be fired if they tried to do the same—the list goes on. Anything you do to help your family . . . there is someone whose health, transportation, financial, or work limitations keeps them from doing that same thing. Help them. Befriend them. Become better by knowing them.

- Are you handy with repairs around the house? Someone in your town needs a wheelchair ramp built, a window replaced, a flowerbed cleaned out, or a fire hazard removed. Find them. Serve them. Share your gift with them.

- Are you a consultant? Solve a problem from which you will never benefit. Don't list it on your resume or profit from it in any way. Simply find a need and fill it.

- Are you an engineer? Use the same skills you use all day at work to help solve complex problems in your community. Maybe a low-income neighborhood has a drainage problem that causes flooding. Maybe a "safe house" needs an engineering assessment to add a second story to their building. Maybe a special-needs center could benefit from a more efficient energy source.

- Are you a real-estate developer? Partner with your local Habitat for Humanity to help find good deals on land so they can help more families build homes. Or donate one single lot in your development for a family that could never afford to live there but works more hours and jobs than most of us could imagine. The stability and convenience of your neighborhood could change a family's story for generations, and your bottom line would barely change.

- Are you an architect or builder? Partner with local non-profits who design and build homes, or manage remodels for families who need them. Help them solve their problems more efficiently or at a reduced cost. Or do it just to bring someone joy.
- Are you in a management role at a medium or large company? Take all the things your team does best and add in the philanthropic dollars already being given within your organization to take on a shared project that solves a real problem in your community forever. Looking for an easy way to multiply your impact? Pair up with a passionate but inexperienced local high school or college service organization and teach them how to carry your idea through to the next generation. Talk about creating real transformation!

> Each one of us has talents and passions that would be valuable assets to share with the world.

I hope you can see how broadly these ideas can be applied to any of us. Each one of us has talents and passions that would be valuable assets to share with the world. Whatever our skill level is, we can find ways to do more good with those competencies.

As for our friend Conner—while he's incredibly talented in marketing and design, he also loves fly-fishing and golf. Could he use those hobbies for his 14 minutes a day? Absolutely. What if Connor and his golfing and fishing buddy (who happens to be his dad) partnered with one of the youth organizations in Detroit to share their passion with kids who might otherwise never have those experiences? What if those youth organizations used this as a reward for their young people with the best attendance or the most service hours? That could create a win-win partnership with a positive ripple effect that stretches far beyond one adventurous weekend enjoying nature.

One of the most surprising and profound aspects of using our creativity to do good for others is that it actually makes us better at our day jobs too. What I mean is that we often get stuck in a rut solving the regular problems we face, and anything outside of those routine solutions feels inaccessible. But doing the kind of good I've listed herein forces us to use new ways of thinking about problems. Like compassion and courage, creativity is a muscle that grows as we use it. We become better at accessing these gifts by forcing ourselves to use them. It's long been proven that regularly doing good for others makes us happier, more fulfilled, and more grateful overall. So while our motivation for doing good should never be selfish, we can expect to see significant positive changes in our own lives when we choose to regularly and intentionally share our best gifts for the good of those around us.

> Like compassion and courage, creativity
> is a muscle that grows as we use it.

# Join the
# Movement

Our only limitation in our ability to do good is our own lack of compassion, creativity, and courage. Every single one of us has gifts to share with the world. Each one of us has something to offer. In this book alone, I've listed more than a hundred ways people like you and me are making a difference and bringing good to the world. Choose one idea. Try it. Then choose another. Try that one. Over and over again, for the rest of your life. It really is that simple.

We've got a lifetime of good and a globe of people to positively impact. And it can happen by dedicating just 14 minutes a day to do more good. But the key is that we start *today* because the only way forward is forward.

We don't have to look very far to see that our world is in desperate need of more good. Suffering, challenges, and pain are all around us. How will we respond? I hope it is with compassion. Compassion that goes all the way into our gut and makes us feel something. Compassion that helps us love our neighbors, weigh our words, create relationships with those who are different from us, and turn walls into tables. Compassion we feel so deeply it hurts. Compassion we use to help bring relief to the pain of others. This is the choice we have every single day when we swing our feet out of bed and walk out our front doors to face another day. Can we give 14 minutes each day to doing good? Of course we can. But will we? I deeply hope we will.

I have many hopes for each of you who chose to pick this book up and read it. But most of all, I hope that you truly believe you are capable of doing so much more good than you can imagine. You don't have to quit your job or move to another country to do it. It's already within you, and you can create enormous, life-altering, world-bettering transformation in just 14 minutes a day.

This book was your personal invitation to join a global movement of ordinary people like you and me who want to give back, offer their best gifts, and do more good—a collective billion hours of it. That's enough good to fill 24 hours a day, 365 days a year, for the next 114,000 years. That's a whole lot of good. Impossible for any of us to manage alone. But exactly what we will accomplish together.

---

Join the movement and take the 1 percent pledge at
www.abillionhoursofgood.org.
I can't wait to see all the good we get into next.

---